KT-133-279

TOM MAC INTYRE

encountering
new and selected poetry zoe

**NEW
ISLAND**

ENCOUNTERING ZOE – NEW AND SELECTED POETRY
First published 2010
by New Island
2 Brookside
Dundrum Road
Dublin 14

www.newisland.ie

Copyright © Tom Mac Intyre, 2010

The author has asserted his moral rights.

ISBN 978-1-84840-069-6

All rights reserved. The material in this publication is protected by copyright law. Except as may be permitted by law, no part of the material may be reproduced (including by storage in a retrieval system) or transmitted in any form or by any means; adapted; rented or lent without the written permission of the copyright owner.

British Library Cataloguing Data. A CIP catalogue record for this book is available from the British Library.

Book design by Inka Hagen

Printed in Ireland by Gemini International

10 9 8 7 6 5 4 3 2 1

For Celine

CONTENTS

CASTLETYMON
BRANCH
PH

SONNET SEQUENCE – THE FINAL MOTHER-FUCK (PERHAPS)

ACKNOWLEDEGMENTS

are due to the editors of the following publications in
which some of these poems first appeared:
*Agenda, Books Ireland, Cyphers, Irish Pages,
The Faber Book of Irish Verse, The Irish Review,*
and *The Irish Times.*

BLOOD RELATIONS (1972)

THE YELLOW BITTERN

Sickens my gut, Yellow Bittern,
to see you stretched there,
whipped – not by starvation
but the want of a jar;
Troy's fall was skittles to this,
you flattened on bare stones,
you harmed no one, pillaged no crop,
your preference always – the wee drop.

Sours my spit, Yellow Bittern,
thought of you done for,
heard your shout many's the night,
you mudlarkin' and no want of a jar;
at that game I'll shape a coffin,
so all claim – but look at this,
a darlin' bird, downed like a thistle,
causa mortis: couldn't wet his whistle.

Sands my bones, Yellow Bittern,
your last earthlies under a bush,
rats next, rats for the wakin',
pipes in their mouths, an' them all smokin';
Christ's sake, if you'd only sent word,
tipped me the wink you were in a bind,
dunt of a crow-bar, the ice splitter-splatter,
nothin' to stop another week on the batter.

Heron, blackbird, thrush – you've had it too,
sorry, friends, I'm occupied,
I'm blinds down for the Yellow Bittern,
a blood relation on the mother's side;
whole-hog merchants, we lived it up,
carped our *diem*, hung out our sign,
collar'd life's bottle, disregardin' the label,
angled our elbows, met under the table

while *Herself* moaned with the rest –
'Give it up – you're finished – a year' –
she lied, I told her she lied,
my staple and staff was the regular jar;
now, naked proof, this lad with a gullet
who, forced on the dry, surely prayed for a bullet;
no, mates, drink it up – an' piss it down,
warm them worms waitin' undergroun'.

(after the Irish of *Cathal Buí*, 18th c.)

SWEET KILLEN HILL

Flower of the flock,
any time, any land,
plenty your ringlets,
plenty your hand,
sunlight your window,
laughter your sill,
and I must be with you
on sweet Killen Hill.

Let sleep renegue me,
skin lap my bones,
love and tomorrow
can handle the reins,
you my companion
I'd never breathe ill,
and I guarantee bounty
on sweet Killen Hill.

You'll hear the pack yell
as puss devil-dances,
hear cuckoo and thrush
pluck song from the branches,
see fish in the pool
doing their thing,
and the bay as God made it
from sweet Killen Hill.

Pulse of my life,
we come back to *mise*,
why slave for Mc Ardle –
that bumbailiff's issue,
I've a harp in a thousand,
love-songs at will,
and the air is cadenza
on sweet Killen Hill.

Gentle one, lovely one,
come to me,
now sleep the clergy,
now sleep their care,
sunrise will find us
but sunrise won't tell
that love lacks surveillance
on sweet Killen Hill.

(after the Irish of *Peadar Ó Doirnín*, 18th c.)

CATHLEEN

Lovely whore though,
lovely, lovely whore,
and choosy –

slept with Conn,
slept with Niall,
slept with Brian,
slept with Rory;

slide then, the long slide.
Of course, it shows.

(after the Irish of *Eoghan Rua,* 18th c.)

I BAILED OUT AT ARDEE (1987)

THE HILL-FOLK

Your Saturday night chipper releases
amiabilities of steam, truce-

offering fantastical to the May
downpour you would not wish

on the neighbour's child
(just might bring growth),

never fret, resumes in one hour,
there, thereabouts, the ould shnooker,

process to the bars, sip aisy,
humped faces, purr of the baize,

The Championship of The World
subsumes The Mysteries, Ave,

Ave the probable Champ's
six kids and sizeable cheque,

look at that street, terror
how empty a street can be,

the – what is it? – three weeks
now murder remains unsolved,

corpse a renowned practical
joker, gift of rhubarb, stalks

wired sort o' thing,
you could buy a drink

for the killer, forensic boys
up to here in slides,

skin-an'-hair, coat-tails, soot,
cows, someone says, seem happy

enough, promise of grass,
suck the sod, smell breezes,

rump to rump for the heat in it,
piped music from blackbird, linnet,

the same cows'll eat no clocks;
contention ongoing with the village

downstream, certain other localities,
come to that, concerning one

birth-place that cannot be nailed,
The Last of The Harper's;

all know where he's buried,
skelp of a journey away,

that's all known, Big House
he died in, wake, funeral

for days, much-honoured grave,
it's the birth-place, hearth,

spangle of door, well, and tree,
air 'round that first note...

Not *casus belli*, no, but still...
It claws at them, niggles

women an' childher, in special,
they'll swear that he's kin,

aye, show you the spot – Look,
there next the rath, that dip –

skirtin' those whins they've heard
(and who'll doubt their word?)

Ó Carolan's long bony fingers
pluck strings, tap the runes,

from the echoing clay
clay's harsh fevers allay.

RETURN VISIT

There's a sign,
you that's one for signs;
you've climbed the mountain,
gone into the wood
to touch the stones –
the stones can't be found.

Scan the view,
weigh the lean
mid-winter air.

I stand there years,
know-nothing, let
my feet call,
Shantemon wraps me,
the quick shade goes
down like sweet milk,
terre verte of the fir,
red-needle floor,
wand of lemon,
and I am hermit,
lived here years

where five stones
divide the trees.
Pick your step
now in the good
quiet, enter the old
enclosure, how they wait,
wait and move,
light along their shoulders
the underside of light,
this season's word
and sumptuary kiss.

Bathe in that light.
Give them your hand.

SIONNAN

lived under wave,
close to the well
where the fish lived
(don't touch the fish),

well knew the well,
nine streams, nine hazel,
the hazels let fall
leaf, blossom, fruit,
in one go, the fish
gobbled the lot
(don't touch the fish),

at noon, Sionnan
stole to the well,
the fish basked,
plumed, digested nuts,
the fish shone
(don't touch the fish),

she reached, touched,
well rose, streams rose,
the waters pitched her
into the upper world,

end of Sionnan,
start of a river,
well may the river
carry her name.

RENDEZVOUS

Touch on my left shoulder,
the first leaf of autumn,
green as young love,
crossed my breath, knew
the gap in the wall
of the well's ante-chamber
where I stood in water
for the cure of the water,
August gale from south-east,
meanest wind in the sky.

AISLING

Lake-light gathers
the look of my life

returns no word

for her that kiss
slept till now

blue-eyed grass
supple as the bee

far from home

I love her
I want her
I won't breathe

her name

DAUGHTER SONG

Friend and Lover
and Golden Plover,
come now if you're free,
read the locks,
make the sign,

food on the table,
immersion's piping,
your eye's my reason,
your colour's my why,
your wing's the season
the seasons untie,

(you've crossed The Shannon
once or twice, ever hear
'Purr go the apples,
Peesh-weesh go the trees'?),

o, wonder within
and wonder without,
break into my home,
crowd into my heart.

from
FLEURS-DU-LIT (1990)

HOME PLACE

Rime on the pane,
spittle-and-thumb,
spittle-and-thumb,
the glass clears,

snow on the lawn,
the trees, familiar
trees, night quiet
something else again,

the glass blurs,
spittle-and-thumb,
spittle-and-thumb,
the glass clears,

the snow, the lawn,
the trees, dispose
inalienable quiet,

December gift
for December man,
spittle-and-thumb,
rime on the pane.

SEASIDE

Ebb-tide, the fisherman's step
says – 'Work done, the work begins,'

he enters a shore pool,
spear-stick poised, strikes
twice, sets the fish
by the pool's edge...

I know you, and I don't,
when you surface again
in the choral last of the day,
sea-urchin and wishbone
and tousled undine,

'But I'm explaining' – that's you,
isn't it, 'I'm *explaining*, dammit,'

isn't that you, Love, isn't it,
isn't it, isn't that you?

THE PURPLE FLOWER

The purple flower
sprig of a thing
finding a way

the purple yields
underplumage
first feathering's
indolent down

the purple frees
purple on fire
tourbillon deeps
fire the purple

the petals move
five to the flower
as one they move
purple and fire
one in the weave

SKYLINE

Hunter well-weathered,
you with such flair
for the clean kill,
have you considered
cross number four
on your afternoon hill?

CANDOUR OF THE WELL

The table set
for one, the bowl –
your *fruits-de-terre*,

where berry stares
at candle-end,
and candle-end
gives back the stare.

SOMEWHERE ELSE

Somewhere else the eagle
bred the whirlwind;

where we lay,
the one-strand river

was midnight nurse
and dawn's delay;

we heard eels whistling
in heaps of the deep,

we slept under
the sound of the tide
and the seagulls' feet.

SHE

Unleavened bread leavens
my well-travelled tongue:
near the altar a spring:
votive redwood spade infers
the husbandry of breathing.

Here's the beat of arrival,
here the heft of return,
here the vision candle,
here the gown ne'er torn...

You'll know my step.
She departs for the fields,
Mother of The Plants,
Daughter of The Deep-Dish Leaves.

TOCCATA

Today's *Irish Times*,
inside page, lower half,
presents a beautiful poem,

half-page bare bar
this one poem, it
has all the space
in the wide world,

note, in that regard,
short lines galore –
you may mould these

recklessly, that's allowed
since here's no ordinary
poem, 'Compose as you read'
is the chosen form,

by no means easy
but, get accustomed, you'd
have it no other way,

lines shape or melt,
stir, firm, alter,
all hangs on you, on
your lips, eyes,

bedizened breath, the yield
is flux, contained,
soft as a thigh,

and the poem's about?
It's about the colours
which famously embellish
The Book of Hours,

some liberty to quote
from such a poem,
'Compose as you read'

is no trivial pursuit,
and yet two lines,
two lines follow me,
won't let go,

lines such as these
must be spoken, I know
the voice, no one

speaks the least like you,
I've met no one meets
words quite your way,
who else would aver,

offer to the faint of heart –
'For a long time now I've
felt your lips on mine.'

BABY IN THE FIRE

Tickle an ear,
he hops up and down
like an egg in a ponger,

I'm The Monsoon-Horse,
hums the clear of his eye,
I'm The Martinmas Gander,
I sleep like a thrush,
I don't look at calendars,
I'm your permanent bash,
and The Patron of Hauliers.

Pause (mine) for breath.
The smile on offer's – earth-lit.
Look, he points, Look at –
in the park opposite
a row of horse-chestnut
bursts into leaf,
There's foliage, Mister,
if it's foliage you're after.

Leaves of two colours
invite us, envelop us,
That child's a flamer,
sings the green, sings the yellow,
Make your shoulder his pillow,
sings the green, sings the yellow.

THE SEA POTATO

My love brings
a sea potato, heart-
urchin of the lower shore,
modestly sand-coloured
with soft backward-
pointing spines: no teeth,
she asserts, who has well
perused her *objet trouvé*,
the versatile spines pass food
to the pert mouth,
and, she is not slow
to display, the sea
potato is singularly petalled,
her pliant index finger
explores, reveals, five
dorsal petals, anterior
extending a sibilant
auxiliary southward groove –

Smell, she says: fume,
fume of salt furrows,

Listen, she says, places
against my ear the soft
sand-coloured thing:
arpeggios, misted, ten
thousand shells chime
in the waves' undertow.

from

A GLANCE WILL TELL YOU
AND A DREAM CONFIRM (1994)

KISSES

Would you like to hear
of the kisses we share?

Track of The Sanderlings,
Hide-an'-Seek of The Swallow,
Yellow-Hammer-and-Tongs,

Tit's Morning Milk,
Linnet Reflecting, Sweet
Sleep of The Thrush,

Swift Going South, Take
Your Fill of The Thermal,
Streak of The Kingfisher,
Golden Plover Wheels The Shore –

nights like tonight,
Lord, how they play,
as The Summer Triangle
folds The Milky Way.

RSVP

Urbanely leppin'
out of his skin,
frog wonders would
I care to dine?
Cucumber sandwiches,
pears, prickly or plain,
table-cloth sap-green
of the alfresco world.

'I'm the one,' says
frog's bright eye, 'or
have you forgotten,
amn't I the one
who laid it down –
No need for hammer
in the rainy season?'

MARCH, ERRISLANNIN

Jupiter minding The Twins,
Venus blithe in the west,
my love yawns, reclines,
'Weight of desire,' she says –

that suffices,
the house capsizes;

vernal now
the curlew's cry,
vernal find us
where we lie.

PANGUR *EILE*

Within my dream
I watch you sleeping,
am shown your dream,

my eyes widen
to a cat couchant,
snake for piping,

cool periphery,
head and tail
meeting by the cat's

tail, on the cat's
head a small bird,
I take my fill

of this picture, pray
it may endure,
it has more to do,

the cat couchant
is first to go,
next the piping,

the snake sloughs
itself, the bird's left,
the bird dissolves

to just the head,
head to an eye,
the eye holds

mine, the eye's gone;
still dreaming, I rouse
you from sleep

to tell – everything,
that in my dream
I watched you sleeping –

your eyes widen –
saw your dream,
how it played

there, all the keys,
and lightest touch,
you hold me close

(that bird's eye),
hold me, hold me,
we continue sleeping.

SMALL HOURS

The red cat knows
and lets you know
everybody knows

nothin' open
two in the morning
except legs.

That's why she's here;
besides, she's got
squatter's rights.

Don't stare – her
bloodless red's
tricky to breathe –

where, where are you,
love, at the other
end of my tether?

The red cat waits,
could wait forever,
all she wants

is liver and lites,
when you say when,
not till then.

À bientôt.
The red cat melts,
furls to afterglow.

À bientôt.

STORIES OF THE WANDERING MOON (2000)

VERTIGO

That sleepless
abundant
neglected
ora pro nobis
heather pink:

colour of your
labia exactly as
your lipstick –

for a moment,
call it years,
I'd no notion
where to look.

THE CRY

The cry rose, tangled
her breath, found a way,
bawled, sobbed, wept,
faltered, resumed,
louder, wilder...

Shameless, bidden,
she became her tears,
let the flood take
what course it would,
she glistened, shone,
gathered light until,
this side *Amen*,
I could not tell
ma belle from waterfall.

She looks up, contrite,
streaked, biting
an unruly lip: reach,
hold close, comfort;
lumpish, welcome her
from The Land Under Wave.

THE CARPENTER'S DAUGHTER

Well, since you ask the question,
she was the carpenter's daughter
fair. The father's workshop surely
figured: abundant coffins,
spirit-levels that rang clear,
peachy fuzz of the sawdust,
and, glory of the *mise-en-scene*,
wood-shavings to the knee –
odorous innocent unregenerate
flux, out of which stepped
Celia, black hair *flagrante*,
complexion an unlikely, thrilling,
prelapsarian *café au lait*.

Would she like to play Doctor?
The chosen didn't have to be led,
gave – *soignée* – the mortal nod.
We made, at speed, for my abode,
detached, spacious, somnolent.
I take her to a neat west-
ward facing room known as –
a former occupant's profession —
'The Surgery'. *Gaudeamus*.

The game of '*Doctor*', for two
concerned practitioners, organ-
ises itself at a buoyant lick.
Swathe a willing table
in an expansive rug – or rugs,
your seraglio curtains will caress,
all sides, the humbly assistant
floor. Pause. Admire the work.

No one knows where we are.
No one guesses our mission.
We enter our well of shadows.
Celia reclines. And is bare
to the waist, no least action
required on her part – or mine.

We are both
unconscionably calm.
Her thighs muse in the dusk.
My gaze opens
to the wink between.
Now it comes,
an odour, odours,
odours of Celia
Celia adorning.

HOLD-ALL

The bag you carried
when we first got together –

I've watched that bag
crimp, gather quiet,
shift, sudden as soot.

Could take you to see it –
asleep in a cupboard,
caught in a sun-trap,
looking out of a tree,
the brink of a smile...

WAITING

Timid with hunger,
bit of a ghost
from your summer
in that vestibule.

Tomorrow we'll visit
the settling grave.
Today? Today we've
wit sufficient
to hold till night.

So: eye each other,
swap words, stories,
come morning share
a tousled wreath.

BONHEUR d'ESCLAVAGE

Her panties not quite
dry shimmy in the hot
air-flow from the blower's
antic overdrive,

cream nothings, lace
somethings – 'Soit vite!' – quiver,
hornpipe, foxtrot, hand
it to Bo Diddley,
Bo The Man

they couldn't put down –
'Ça va?' 'Bien, très bien' –
we resume flight, spell
figures of eight (while
the blower rhymes
satisfaction), take off,
endeavour fresh lifts,
pirouettes, extensions,
demand an audition,
right now, at The Kirov...

October sun fills
our disordered lair,
the panties a pennant,
Bo Diddley and I
the breast of a linnet,
ma belle en retard,
brushin' the hair,
ironin' a blouse,
changin' her shoes.

LANCELOT du LAC

Les contes de la lune vague
après la pluie has just gotta be
the finest movie ever made,

about love – what else? – and death,
full of mist above water, immodest
dissolves, departures, riddles
of return, houses separating plank
by plank to the sound of bells,
but what I remember most

are the lakes, paternoster and still.
You're a lake, I decided
that night, uncovered, *copain*,
you're a lake, mist plentiful,
a boat seen, lake again
(I monitor rapid-eye motion).

Les contes de la lune vague
apres la pluie – ghost people,
a woman, a man, the flame,
we came home, quiet, by water.
walking on water, the Seine, sister
canals, I thought, What the hell?
Is that a sheep or a pram? A
clochard shouted – 'L'ectoplasma!'

Mizoguchi directed it, and died –
so they say, o, decades back,
Mizoguchi's not dead, not a bit,
saw him attendant as we
meandered, looked like
Utamaro, Kawabata, the woman
who wrote that pillow-talk
book – or was she heathen Chinee?

My lake *copain*, mist,
boat seen, mist again,
must rapids be our portion?
Separations? Crumbling
to a sound of bells?

Well, we're here to learn,
it's been said (too often).
The moon lying back on its heel,
Orion's belt only, the pair of us
telling over and over *Les contes
de la lune vague apres la pluie*...

A CERTAIN ROOM

Is it true
that in a certain
room of the castle we always
love the once beloved?

Where's that room?
On the seventh floor!

Once a lifetime
you may by accident
or prayer or unsolicited gift
discover it,

shed the maze,
astonished stand.
Everything as was.
And more. And more.

from
ABC (2006)

OPEN HEARTH
for G

Peeler-size, *Eduardus Rex*,
still warm from the blaze,
Pat the Yankee lugged home
the tongs like a bad debt.

The Yankee moved on, the tongs
fell to a rogue blacksmith,
furnished his long left arm.
They sowed the blacksmith in time.

Up on thirty years
the tongs lay propped in a shed,
summer a squeak of swallows,
winter slavish, slavish out.

Wrist supple over turf and scantling,
my love now plies the tongs,
touch, stroke, stir, nudge,
silken endearments, then fire.

BUDDY

The dog catches
quartz light
of the mountain rim,

day so clear
you could reach out,
touch his coat,

no telling when
he'll come home but
he'll come home,

your *solide gaillard*,
map in his eye
of your Slievemore.

WIDDA

You must tell the bees
the bee-keeper is dead...

Sunday, an ass's heat,
she approached the orchard,
took the path to the hives.

Low din of the business:
she watched the smart bundles
arrive loaded, enter, un-
load, leave on the wind
that was no wind, a wave,
suspended, knew again
the honey, comb, way
he'd present it – *Yours, Mary*,
let her taste-buds travel
heather-honey, clover-honey,
honey warbling the rose...

She'd shut eyes to pray,
sip tay from a saucer,
bring word to the bees –
Thomas, your keeper, is dead.

She stood there, she looked,
was aware of the bees'
to-and-fro, and next
she saw him, head veiled,
move through the trees –
he moved bolder than life –
her chest thumped good-bye,
the light bee-keeper stride
became one with the haze.

DOWN SKI-PISTES OF GOSSAMER THE GOLDFINCHES CAME

ripped open the seed-bags,
rode stalk, stem,
leaves that wère, air,
side-saddle, pillion,
flying trapezium, arsy-
versy – o, my beauty,

there's one cool gent,
wisp of down the beak adorning,
You're a Chinese painting, friend,
down takes wing –

meadow, haggard,
mill, table,
the thistle's on fire,
the goldfinches – somewhere,
a toucan, a cancan,
an anything-you-can,
the whole world seed,
it's now o'clock –

blink: all over,
bar gold of their slipstream,
pan for that, lover.

LA LANGUE d'OISEAUX

Wakeful soul-bird leads
the dawn-chorus hours
before it's due, a note
more than human

lifts, insists, *prima*
donna assoluta, audience
won switches tack: moves now
her sumptuous silent song –

leopard-skin halter, simmers of,
about the breast of a missel thrush
I know, have gotten to know,
these morning days of spring.

SO THERE NOW

She has the advantage,
she's here to see you,
yet silkily indifferent...

Please don't stay long –
she won't, she won't, time
enough, merely, to let
you salute that plump red,
her state of being, mind,
measureless – not
to cramp it – estate.

Moue. Conversable
perk of the snout – 'I
know you play golf, friend;
I know the temptation
to kiss the lost ball,
I am, after a fashion,
the lost ball. I've had
too much of the rough.'

And goes mum. Teases
a strand of whisker. Red rat
in the full of her health.
The ghost of an eye
allows, 'I'm dangerous lonesome.
Came here from Chester
with Caesar's Ninth Legion,
the one got lost in the rain.'

Red against spring green.
You saw St Patrick raise
some, fell more. 'Be assured,
they won't rhyme me
to a watery end. Lots,
lots, jejune suitors, have tried.'

She rolls on the grass,
frivols ballerina claws –
'Pardon my French,' she says,
'You could be – up to you –
entirely – my next *macédoine*.'
'So you're not carnivorous?'

A hit? And a miss. Just
watch her stretch the pause...

THE MESSENGER

Breeze, they say, through the keyhole,
that's you. Imperious quiet, tangible,
in the liveliest room. Cat-ice. An oven
ablaze. Windfalls of love on

the Zuyder-Zee. And you're violet-
haired, like The Muses. I know
it was you, light-footed, led me
to that temple, night of growthy rain.
A tiled floor, *laudamus*, the Roman
in Ireland, centre-piece a jewel:
circle, within the circle sweet hound
on the gallop, outline – tail
to snout – oval, oval-shaped leaf
one with the wind. I've a handful
of such-shaped leaves, the green,
the withered. You, you're around.

'Lose them.' High Infant, I throw
the leaves. Directed, radarless,
rogue, the leaves fly, drift
to the floor. Blossoms an oval cameo,
the hound, lambent, seasons in flow.

GHOST AT THE FEAST
for M

It's a kind of lust in reverse,
the sonneteering anorexic perverse.

Early in the proceedings, a supporter
says, unaffectedly, 'You had to show.'
The answer is in The Infirmary, find
Bureau of Affirmative Action, ask for
St Sebastian, fresh from The Battle
of Little Big Horn, porous Sebby topping
latest chart of the (halo'd) unwanted,
therefore, *bunoscionn, entrée* so long
as you settle for berth in far billabong
of ghost dimension, that ethereal
note en marge declare anthem,
flag, and gild your stoic phlegm.

Din. Buzz-crackle. Incitements.
Wised-up, sip *Select* mineral water,
play profile games, test obliquities,
taut as the bee, float a foot,
foot-and-a-half, say, above ground.
Everyone, but everyone, knows you're
here. Most keep a distance. Contagion
of the other world, people are not

that slow. Ever been ghost at the feast
before? No. Perhaps. Fair to record,
she did say to me once, 'Always
something about you,' she comes
out with, 'of The Wraith at The Ford.'
Pulled, pliant, from her sybil-hoard.

Everything, Sir, now happening.
Stressful, sure stressful, but never
doubt the propriety of your presence,
impropriety, neck, cheek, other cheek,
sybaritic weightlessness – *give over*!

Her melodiously haunted sister spots
you, flashes piratical alliance. Her
kid-brother appears, hazed, his wont,
in deprivation, and, stung, you
recall a recurring weather of hers.
'Summer Cloud,' you'd tease, shadow
nuzzling the slopes, on the move,
melted, back again, configuration
altered. Moment, as ever,

comes from nowhere, Ankara,
The Fifth Army, random swish
of the tail of a desert fox. She's
within ten metres of you. You're
talking, and not, to X,Y, Zuleika
Dobson. Eight metres. Zap. Poor
back, truthfully, half-towards her,
graph, *pia mater* to big toe, subtle
veer of her flight-path to enter
convenient and obliterating fields
of babble, and you are, lick

this dust of the imperative, sweepstake
twist of a leaf, last of autumn,
first, unheralded first of spring,
transparent, iridescent, speckled,
being blown across the bows
of The Maudelayne, kissing mainsail,
topsail, spinnaker, settling on
the gunwale, mercy of spray,
luck, ebb-tide, and gibbous moon.

Months later, meet her, husbanded,
in a penthouse of dream. Let
your heart beat the curtain's brocade,
cool in a corner. Lunch? Dinner?
Coffee? She encodes your chronic fever,
won't say Yes, doesn't say No, is
utterly herself, munificent.

BRIDGIE CLEARY

I love, love, the stir o' company
ye can't see, it spakes of other
dominions, not that far
distant, men an' women tall
in silks an' sarsenets, organdie,
takin' the air or, come nightfall,
switchin' to their flaunty

daisybells, fondlin' other to a waft
o' notes, them notes audible, o, yes,
audible, be sure, to Bridgie Cleary,
aye, an' manys the Bridgie Cleary,
from 'ithin their Glens o' Quiet
or their ivy-walled demesnes.

THE CLOWN

for TH

Beware the clown, that portable
hatched grimace testament
to appetites unappeasable,
one taste worse than another,
you, you're worst of the lot,
get – *Basta!* – out of his sight.

But give him – *Merci, merci* –
the music, make-up, lights,
sweat, sawdust, razzmatazz,
and, font of voluptuary grace,
he ravishes you, you and yours,
with tender fingers lifts the veil,
most tenderly allows it fall.

You go home shriven, forsaken.
Where on earth have you been?
You've been to bed with the clown,
the huckster, hoaxer, shaman.
Don't ask him how it's done.
Himself again, he can't tell.
The veil, just. Lifted. Let fall.

SLIEVE GULLION

You've reached the summit, there's
the lake all the talk was about,
slap on top, an eye, it stares
back at you – 'Hello' – innocent.

The fawn, seems, led Fionn up here,
into the lake – her scut's a wand –
hero emerges 'three days later',
mop matt white that was blond,

should she meet you, that fawn
will say – 'Your hair's long white,'
and bockety three-score-and-ten
won't, for once, have answer pat.

Hellovan education already;
third-way up the mile climb
to the shabby cairn (just slid upsy-
downsy off it), I utter the crime

of looking back, ten counties
and a tranche of sea possess me,
suction plasmic, custody of the eyes
thereafter, Enclosed Order Custody,

that'll I'arn ye. Should mention,
caught the sound (same dunt)
of the mountain, feral, atropine,
felt – God's truth – arteries dilate,

o, one bonny bony clarion. Pass,
friend. Reconnoitre. From cairn
northward to the lake's a mess,
bog, bog-hole, lake worn

now, lonesome, wants *someone*,
asks – aches – engagement,
'Gullion,' they say, from *Dhubh Linn*,
'the black pool,' she'll stir, tantrum,

threap recognisances
down your throat should you deny
her due regard, *Lá eile*, Petals,
and I mean that, haven't I

made obeisance to the *genius
loci*, met you – we *have* met;
furthermore, a shower threatens,
wicked fond of the rain, call it

quits for this pilgrimage,
wave to the lake, start the descent,
facilis decensus but for drag
of the vista, knees on the spit,

a quaternity takes my fancy,
vista's maw one with sound
of the mountain, both, intimately,
kin to the lake, all tied

to the fawn, The Ineluctable Fawn,
'Your hair, Sir, is years white' –
'But in your power, Gentlest One,
to alter that, transform every last

rib...' Untutored lips, I doubt
my tongue would dare the words.
Stumbled here on the ascent, don't
worry, you're fine bar the knees,

they're cooked. Blessed tree-line.
An apple (organic). Mineral water
(still). And a wavering elation.
Drive west. Summer's an empire.

Umpire. What inveigled you the day?
The mother lived for the road,
stiffer she got. The father, easy,
did sums, watched light fade

as it fades now on drumlin
duck-eggs, greeny-bluey in surcease
of August. Watershed of the Erne.
Mark of the planter, bountiful trees.

Home. By the fire. One quiet
house. Key in the door, man,
a poor housekeeper. And yet.
Table spread, breathes the wine.

Empire. Umpire. Down to the wire.
OED, open mouth, close eyes,
flip the pages, roam finger,
see what The Powers'll send yiz;

free-fall finger finds *Endark*,
meaning 'to render dark, to dim,'
after that, parenthetical, *Very rare...*
OED aside. A touch. She came.

Bats delineate the garden.
Good to get out now and again,
consult augurers, their finial claim.
And Gullion, wet snout of Gullion,
recommend you to all my children.

ENCOUNTERING ZOE

Avoid the unforced error,
honeyed *faux pas*, of asking
the former, years later, to send,
if no trouble, some shots of your
time together, scarcely a word exchanged
since, so what, people meet, hills don't,
she will respond –

            and then some.
The envelope arrives, lightweight,
such restraint, *she* doesn't figure,
of the handful one matters, one
jumps the years, life to come.
It's a shot, the hand pales,
of you, happiest man by far
in the ring of Ireland, shot
taken, early seventies, by a genius
Russian poet who died young, it shows:
the subject – backdrop of rocks, ocean –
is haunted, and in love; better,
haunted *by* love, that rare
(comparitively) condition, ter-
minal, sure, they're working on it,
I believe –

            Grab time out. Phone
to say thanks, mention (*de rigeur*)
your stake in that particular shot,
cock the starveling bothered ear.
It harvests intake-of-breath-cum-
sibilant, tapering, beyond analysis –
O, bagel-baby of my salad days, O,
lox and gefilte fish of lazy Sabbath noon –
we two made a view of islands,
lighthouse beam, we made more,

there was a garden took the eye,
her, a wonder, carrying our mite
the few brave months – and gone –
April mishap, dim quiet after
in which beats *maxima culpa*,
did you sufficiently delight,
do you, will you, some day, never,
give blood to the wishing-well?

Oceans west, she's thinly clad,
25 today, Finger-Lake District,
cool buzz back of her inaud-
ible, encyclical, mastic: she
explains, daughter Zoe's Conferring,
an occasion, some friends around,
Zoe's, theirs...Yes, that time of year,
Latinate scroll, deckled, ribbon-
bound, reach, let your hand
touch, caress, the furled oblong.
Zoe, dear near-relation. '*Sé*
do bheatha, Zoe. I bow to a mother,
to a daughter grown, retreat
to the shades where I belong.

THREE-FACED IDOL & FRIEND

The cheeky first face is setting out,
young man's wide gaze, aperture
mid-mouth lisps the breast known,
salutes lips, breasts, clits of the soon-
to-be. Reared far from the hind tit,
and wearing – look – near to a grin,
our hero (all arrangements in place)
will collect, his due, the hero portion.
He tightens, then loosens, his belt:
farewell lactic slopes of innocence,
welcome vales awash with cuntal juice.

Second face has been to the wars,
what've you lost, Dad, lost or found,
that won't permit some hurt to mend?
Dad, child, can't hear the question,
there's a ruckus jars his very bone;
interrogate him till Trumpet Sound,
he'll keep to himself his swag of scars;
let be, child, his eye's on Silence,
Soldier's home, home from the wars,
valleyed Silence his final stand.

The third face is visor brow, down-
cast eyes. Gravity's heft. An old man,
affairs in order, pokes the clay,
drumlin moist, deems it friendly,
hears it list, absorb, minutiae
of seven decades' deed, misdeed,
mingled yarn, standard portion –
'Thru'-other walk, but your own.'
From the clay, the visor-brow,
fair greeting, handshake, nod,
for that stripling poised alongside,
dying to turn the virgin ground.

Alter the light. Now d'ye mind.
The poll – fat lump – is harvest
moon, no end to her largesse,
merry-go-round, sorry-go-round –
She Who Swans It On The Milky Way,
Heifer, Bullin' Cow, The Dun,
how she embraces all our faces,
me bucko, soldier, pantaloon,
how she gathers all our chassis
as she melts the lock of stasis,
Hera, Isis, *is Tusa, Bó Fhoinn*,
hail your hoof-prints, teemy bed,
the bright *bainne*'s buoyant flood,
Ould Wan on the slopes of Glan'
cries out – 'She gave till she bled!'

And Mad Sweeney had this to say
(Sweeney who died lappin' the milk),
'There has, perhaps, been too much talk,'
he didn't look in the least *ar strae*,
'Imagine. Imagine till you glisten,
glisten big-time, beautiful as May.
That's the milk. Milk's Imagination.'

Love that Sweeney! *Milk's Imagination*!

TRAVELLERS

for Lia & Dan

Once upon a time
in nineteen-ninety-nine – forward
granddaughter, nigh on seven,
stories spill out of her hand,
words the one and only cure:
she's vexed, say, bitchin',
send for *fáinleog, dibble, siffleur...*

Grandson, ten, no dunce,
haunts the wood, tuned to listen,
test that maze. Returned, he'll talk
badger's bone, spoor of mink,
vixen's love-note wild. Once
met hen-harrier's stare –
'Raptors,' you're told, 'don't blink.'

Dare I give them my choice
latest from the windfall shore?
Head, ears hittin' high C,
conversable head of the hare.
Body's alongside, poor paltry
costume. The audible silence.
The within – *'Allons-y, allons-y!'*

TWO HORSES

Of a terrible early, early spring,
waited for me on grandmother ground
fine Dove-Grey, honest Injun brown,
Dove-Grey's more, more nor mortal thing.

Doldrum forties, meet them again
on a slope above the randy sea.
An old fisherman ripe in his skin –
'Brown's for races, the prize,' March dawn,
horses' breathing, 'But our friend Dove-Grey...'

Seventy plus, return to the grandmother
spot. House tossed, farm's a kip.
From the yard where that stable was,
Dove-Grey, hour come, dances,
bridled, saddled. And Child Wonder's up.
A wave, waves, we two go backaways.

Child Wonder calls – 'Room for another.'
Only the one answer. I'm aboard,
Child's in my arms, we canter, gallop,
Dove-Grey, mane singing, seizes the road.
This is the road was always there.
It's early, terrible early, of an early spring,
all of us more, more nor mortal thing.

BOUQUET OF DAFFODILS

I was surprised – I was shaken –
such balanced wooing in the gesture –
green of the stalks soft April green,
blossoms cloth-of-gold to die for.

Lying there on the broad of my back –
what is it about the offer of flowers,
you half-asleep in the sack?
Study, sustain, a novel deference...

'And did you fear her summons?'
someone asked. When Proserpina
presents to you her daffodils, Yes
is the only wear, *a chroí*. La Divina

arrived, delivered, melted –
leaving her signature, & something else:
stretched there, bouquet in my hands,
Spring and Winter the one juice,

I'm filled, fuelled, with the flavour
of Her style, savvy, gentleness –
the good Demetrian drop in her;
comes again that stir of gentleness,
the like of which we know not here.

SCISSORS

For the visit, thank you;
Lady Proserpina, no doubt
you've heard, came by of late
(Royal Highness with daffodils),
Old Charon fingers his list,
my diet's roses and rue.

For your present, thank you,
present, earnest, warrant,
the works. Ambience, I greet,
uneven dirt floor, lee
of the kitchen sink, no frills,
modest signature coup.

Wrap-up, Atropos, thank you:
we take aboard the scissors'
mint complexion: ever in use,
snip-snip, snippety-snip,
they shine, Lady, your bladed
hansel, justly, shines as new.

EAGLE

The hills again, the amorous hills,
vigilante eagle again on the prowl:
hunters about, gunfire peals,
I step into my only Gospel.

Eagle lands topside of a ditch,
today's plumage many's a colour,
claret, myrtle, peach, amethyst.
Without looking, he strips me bare.

What is it you want, I wonder?
Everything. Nothing. All I have.
You've never worn these robes before,
ambassador mine from The Cliffs of Love.

A loose tension. An idle storm.
Don't light a match between us.
He maps a road, surveys a kingdom,
still won't lend me his gaze.

Pinions royal urge, Leap.
Learn, Child, to earn. To yearn.
Was my sticky caul this gom's cap?
The buzz: the buzz is High Noon.

He won't loiter, that I know.
Frolicky, the hills attend our parley.
Eyes absent. But the talons see.
And a feather sings – 'I've called you.
What, tell us, do you call me?'

DARK ANGEL'S HAND

Caravaggio black, inly lit,
his right hand, pontiff thumb,
grips the blanket, asserts claim –
Come, thou art flesh, thou hast
overcome thy mighty entertainment.

Never met a hand like this,
large, shapely, mandarin, wise;
honest broker, cool *fonctionnaire*,
it admits neither mercy nor ruse.
Look: quick fade. Just a reminder.

Artist's hand, I've revised since,
inscribes the law purely as song:
dulcimer melts to an anvil blaze,
ribboned swallow returns the ring,
the compass note is *rendezvous*!

Hand there. Gone. See you soon.
Getting to know Prince *Aide-Memoire*,
falling, maybe, for his lordly line,
the pair of us blossom low-key wonder,
my state troubles the surround.

Beautiful women brim intent,
well they read what's going on,
how difficult it is, how difficult
to bow the head, whisper *Amen*,
kiss that black, inly lit.

RECENT POEMS

THE GROOM'S VISION

On your way to the wedding,
fell, trim, secure carriage for
a young fir tree, don't fret,
few will notice, those who do
comprehend, stand that fir
in giddy heart of the throng,

address the gilded slippers
directly in your path, bright
summons on finely shaven grass,
they're yours, fatefully yours,
inhabit them now, gift
out of all the stories, Jesus,

one slipper expires in flame,
again few notice, those who do
ingest, you become an airy room
the day explores, this isn't elegy,
tragedy, 'underdeveloped comedy',
fire is every slipper's maiden name,

whisht, The Bride, armoured,
rides past, to her left the legend
river of her being, watch that river,
its nubile stir, heralds tending,
greet your Sovereign, robed
for battle, bearing weightless gold.

A DAY OUT

'The entire day, evening most of all,
was beautiful. We came home quietly,
easily, pausing for a sup of whiskey
in Power's public house. At the weir
of O'Brien's Mill there's a waterfall,
an island of sallies, another of fir.
The Widow's daughter, limber Margaret,
stood between me and the waterfall.
She began to sing, fairy woman
free in winding mist of the falls;
she stood there, sang without let,
notes, believe you me, to frecken
the brave, words to humble the wise.
The Widow Barr wore almost-a-smile.
Blood-red clouds over Slievenamon,
now yellow, blue, black, then jet;
the singing ceased, fairy-woman still.'

(after the Irish 19th c.)

MAGGIE BARR

Went for a long walk with Maggie Barr,
she whom I've christened Semper-Song
(notes all the sweeter for being unaware).
Often shrouded from the light of day,
we rambled summer, wood and grove,
and constantly the birds, the birds sang
in unison with singing Maggie Barr.

In a small valley we lost our way,
no telling now points of the compass,
the needle spun, underfoot – mystery,
that glen left us nearer, nearer by far.
We came out of it, viewed each other.
'I'm fair jaded,' said singing Maggie Barr.
'Two of us in it,' I replied, 'Let us
stretch our limbs on green of the moss.'

Fell asleep she did, happily the wind
played with singing Maggie's untied hair,
revealing a neck white as the hand
of an angel; rowan-berry those lips,
maiden-dew on mine; breasts, compare,
say, wave-at-play on The King's River;
pert waist, tidy little ass a cluster –

two bastard snipe drum from a swamp
lodged to our left – they put an end
to singing Maggie's conversable sleep –
curse o' God on every snipe across the land,
their clatty breed and scuttery seed.
We rose from our bed, discovered a lane,
wandered for home, her arm in mine,
head on my shoulder, eyes on the ground.

(after the Irish 19th c.)

85

'SENT'

Dainty slang, it means 'sent
to heaven, bliss.' Granddaughter
is sent on foot of a white
laying hen (pure-bred) bapt-
ised, breathless kindergarten flair,
'Oriel.' Oriel! To be sure,

she's sent, fowl everywhere, hears,
all weathers, a busty cock crow,
is well aware the fox wears
knives for teeth, can't say no,
he won't breach *this* hen-run,
war declared on Reynardine.

Sent. Heaven-sent. Knew from
day one that child was sent,
give a deal for her wisdom,
doors flung wide, to be sent
on finding a hen-egg, sum
of plenty, shy in the straw, warm.

THE POTION

And this time the potion, surely, is dread.
Against ravelled blue, he sways, content,
states – 'I grant we're close, indeed, yet world,
worlds, apart.' (The cradle of *dread* Skeat

allows a riddle, never said scholar truer
word.) We are now three, companion
arrived. Teasing eddies, the pair loiter.
Feats apocryphal, these birds stare the sun,

more, yield their plumage to that furnace,
souse in the perennial spring, resume
the round, whole again. Fall on your knees,
why don't you, mutt, haven't they come

with provender? Fall! Your neck's stiff,
heart blubber. Aloft the two preserve
arcane proprieties, assure me pelf
is nothing. I agree, for now. I have

agreed before, ancient wound our howdydo.
Will it one day mend? Templed silence
the adagio of their going, westward view
beckons them away. I stand here, flinch.

AND TALKING OF SKEAT,

given what he has to say under *dream*,
you could live on one meal a day,
it means, let us rejoice, a *sweet sound*,
music, *harmony*, and *joy*, *glee*,
besides, the sense of *vision* isn't found
in earliest English but no fret, Skeat's
licensed trawl thru the salt-bleached
North, rummage of The Lowlands Low,
routes us, serendipitous and not, to
The Black Forest, guts of the heartland,
Walpurgisnacht, and dream as *phantom*,
the blood, *sotto voce*, screeches, time
perhaps, for glaciers again, we're in Ultima
Thule (have you been?) to meet, this
was written, the *ghost* who owns the word,
The Good Doctor takes all in his stride,
do I envy him, yes, I do, such upper
Saxon lip, angels are on his side,
he has all the luck, imps of The Arabs,
look at this now, tann'd putti, whisk him
away southward, he has earned respite,
and it's not denied, find him parlour'd in
Persia, poise undiluted by hookah fumes,
and offering, *mens sana*, dream as
deceit, as, to conclude, downright *lie*,
well, as I said, and say it again,
blessed are they with whom angels walk,
not my good fortune, the lean damn'd
are my companions, our eyebrows meet,
mention *dream*, and enter, stage left,
Merlin's gamboge cackle from bottle-green
of an endless wood, hear that music,
friend, you've learned to shiver, once

in a dream I was bidden – 'Raise
your right hand for The Unicorn.' No
great matter, let it lift, seconds
bell'd, gap opened, years, the gesture
wasn't in me, I'm not over it yet.

THE INVISIBLE BALL

Fastest field-game in the known world,
the hurlers go for it, pumped, teeth bared,
the style, the feints, marbled meat & muscle,
but I see only the invisible ball,

can't take my eyes away, I know mine,
varlet pen, white of the patient page,
white of pillowslip, disordered sheets,
variable whites of breathy mortal skin,

the stand rocks, Cats or Yallabellies
a point ahead, I see only muses
mortal or divine attending an eternal
and invisible ball, I move among the dancers,

the music's from a long-deserted island
off the Iveragh Peninsula; Heine, fabled
sieve in his ear, opens every window,
I'm luckiest man in The Ring of Ireland,

all about, is it, deferring to a law,
listen, hosting tonight's invisible ball –
is that Emir – Deirdre – Dervorgilla –
listen to what the woman's saying, 'Na mná,

na mná,' at the invisible ball which is
your life, you are being asked to repeat
thirty-three times per minute, 'Na mná,

na mná,' will you loose that, mean it?
A woman, mortal and divine, takes your hand,
says, 'It's all about bowing to The Law,'
lightly kisses, blessing, your froward lips,
'Morbidezza, per favore, na mná, na mná...'

THE SLOE

Then sleep a while
till in my hand I find
the sloe, studied it, tad
surprised, as one caught
in dream; delicate, to feel
of a finger it opens,
the flesh, softest trumpet,
looked me fairly in

the eye, 'O, taste,' began,
'O, taste and see, lover,
I've been called wry
and worse, don't buy
the half of what you hear.'
Sorcery's shy apprentice,
I am at once obedient,
raise to my lips, taste,
eat, the siren sloe;
a wilding sweetness takes
me, I blossom communicant,

my love enquires, 'And
you enjoyed the sloe?' I
realise they are complicit,
she and the sloe, 'Read
somewhere or other,' she
goes on, 'the same wry
sloe is certain ancestor
of all the purpled plums
ever were or, likely,
ever will. Much maligned,
the dacent sloe.' Inclined
to sport again, we turn
to it, make love to
a band playin', find

ourselves on The Bann
Plain, in that very river,
fishy, aye, fruitful fishy

Bann. Salmon, salmon
of knowledge will swear
we played there, one,
longest day of the year,
in one an' other's arms.

IN AND OUT OF HER DREAM

We're in bed, that atself, only a country
road's the bedroom. A tramp, Arab
complexion, shows. I give him a whiskey,
stiff. Gulp, gone. Next that *Tigress and Cub*

out of all the Blake etchings. And thrawn,
spectre thrawn, her face beside me. 'Don't
stir,' I whisper. They leave us well alone.
Now I regale her with a childhood stunt
but ne'er a happy ever rafter, someone

else's future, not ours: from an upstairs
window I fire an orchid, bold arc
of my covenant, to the Protestant Denise,
blonde shimmer below. The street empties.
'So what's that about?' O, mighty ask!
We know, sortov, The Search is dour work,

rejoice in holy sweat. She's a blue-blood
of Florentine stock, it's fifteen somethin',
Savonarola toast, Ficino Platonic aubade.
'What's,' steadying a moue, 'it all mean?'
More wine, I suggest. She gives the nod,
Chianti a must. Chocolate the vine,
the Tuscan drumlins, our country road,

chocolate the tramp's bowling silhouette.
'My orchid flung to the Planter *belle*,'
I say, 'it's all in that striped vignette,
wish I'd been in your dream to enable
flight of that *cojones* flower, contest
schismy quiet of the purged street, *terrible*,
I wrote once, *how empty a street
can be*...Quoting yourself is truly sinful.
Away into herself she goes, away, away...

SONNET SEQUENCE
THE FINAL MOTHER-FUCK (PERHAPS)

FIND THE LADY

'So did you,' everybody asks, 'find
her?' Yes and No, I answer, mostly Yes,
took years, woeful, to lift the blind
on that window, rude garden, there She was,
here She dances, chameleon *Mistress of Pursuit*;
She'd show stripped, dressed, smile, frown,
will-o'-the-wisp me – gamine of the fanlight,
such perseverance, slow-burn divine,
and silence of Cordelia; piecemeal,
I sought to render her pitapat of love,
comether mudra, 'I'm for you, that's all.
We're bespoke. No horizon our roomy cave.'
Finally, something happens to the weather,
we meet, foot of the stairs, my love-letter
in her hands...

THE INVITATION

He pitched the shoe against the wave, wave
fell away, came back; the second shoe,
wave fell away, came back; he drew
the bait-knife, steadied, hurl'd the knife,
the sea calmed. He got home, man alive,
he got home wishing he could undo
the deed, sat by the fire, hours flew,
knock on the door. 'I'm Treasure-Trove,'
says the man on the pale horse, 'Come
you with me.' A room in the mountain,
her beauty shone. 'Take from my heart
this knife you flung, unholy whirl to maim
predestined love.' He met her Sovereign
eye, shrank, ever after walk'd apart.

SNOW OF ONE NIGHT ONLY

We met in College Green, by Books Upstairs,
white rug underfoot, January day,
the tall Venetian glass the woman bears
is snow to the brim, the season's recipe.
She raises the glass, then leaves. Alone,
I throw myself on the snow, distressed,
clumsy/aware my chalk bones must earn
the next move, shed indolence, be child.
And snow answered: the glass again, mine,
hers. A touch, it's pitta, modest oval,
my coward buds lift to a wheaty tune,
that pitta gulfs me like a charter'd vandal.
And the word Aegis is bending my ear,
and the step, velvet, of the turning year.

THE FINAL MOTHER-FUCK (PERHAPS)

A good baker's dozen present, you
could say we make a meal of it,
musha, why not, this is The Big Split,
not the morning, China, the evening dew.
The guests sit in a circle, concerned to
miss nothing, we gild the transit
toward event coolly, content to target
their flea-market varieties of shoe.
Next, game on, we're coupling, audience
recede, with them least stim of voyeur
cosseting, we enter a shameless sense
of our story, no quarrel, not the colour
of it, no sweat, no flesh, no bone, ghosts
humping, the truth on its chosen salver.

GENEALOGY

Ancestral bohawn's done for, lemon blaze,
expected, a wise wind's promise kept;
sotto voce, the prayer for wise ashes,
the feeling somewhere blood's being let.
Are you a record of remains? Lawn
of The Villa, table d'hôte, reduced trunk
of a young oak, Prince, early mown,
morphs fungi now, lice who'll never lack.
Invisible heave, dazed *amor fati*,
lands you the booley warm above the bay,
abundance of heifers (lowing), grass milky,
a white bull hung like the *Graf Spe*.
Time, perhaps, for a breather. Stare. And stare.
Imagine prints of Europa on the languid shore.

THE OAP

More than satisfied in this space,
a-buzz, tonight's show about to begin,
handful here only, youngish, men,
women, could this be 'the dress'
or, maybe, final run-thru? The design
is mostly shadow, tone, say, violet.
Taking. Now what? The risotto of inert
palpitation covert in Lights Down
sends him, always, yet his cool,
he's quite unconscionably calm, hadn't
looked for this treat, passing thought, idle,
landed him here... Play about to start.
He settles, curious, enters an inland sea,
memory, memories, of the yet to be.

MEIN LIEBLING

You get used to prison, sure, but
the silence, the noise; male/female, grand
recreation, still we wanted out,
escape the biding concern, one plann'd,
well-advanced, more so than we
realise, as sometimes happens, aid
from – how shall I put it – the Maquis
who inhabit the air. That day the yard
formed music, mantic, notes you could
eat, the long-forgotten primordial cuisine,
Jesus, we fed, I shouted– 'Liebestod.'
The cry came, perfect pitch, rune,
O, Word Within The Word, Scorched Angel,
what love-knots resile from dusks of your anvil!

THE ANTLER

The antler which honours our estate
has taken leave, met it this morning,
sturdy linchpin of a bawways gate
up the road, says the antler – 'Livelong's
the name of this field. Enter.' I did,
soft fall to the ground reminds me
of fields once known, hollows, I find
deer grazing, among them, *mirabile
visu*, a blue fawn, several playact
with a hare, I am, at once, adorer
of the blue fawn, we are fiercely met,
never on this earth have I been where
now I lie. In bits. A blue fawn
assembles me. Unknown blue. Mine.

THE SALMON

For intro the umbral keep, the pool,
West of Ireland, our *smidiríní* west,
the fish open wide, reserved, evangel,
hunter stricken, speared, could be ghost.
Courtship begun, the salmon somersaults
for my embrace, embrace that fears
the suitor's kiss; endless jooks, jolts,
I'm beast, breast, hint of sea-breeze.
Sea-Breeze it was one day advised –
'Lived tenderness moves in the water,
always somewhere bent, already arrived,
breathing appointment. Engagement's where
to cast, resolution salmon in the pot.
Got it, man?' 'Almost,' I stutter, 'almost.'

THE FROG

I know this frog like I know kid brother,
harvest frog will put me back on my legs,
special juice they have like no other,
she told me who taught me to suck eggs.
All happens aisy if it's in the script;
the frog, the knife, the well, I'm calm, victim
calm, savant, frog knows what's meant
to be, frog will aid and abet the crime.
Acned subaltern, I stoop to open
the frog's belly, fluent stroke, blood
gouts into the well. And I glimpse a wean,
gism of the blood, water's receptive bride.
Now the well darkens. On bended knees
I wait. I'm told – 'Drink to the lees.'

HARD NIGHTS

The red cat sits on my coffin, glaze
of the opened drumlin, men nodding, women
anxious above their shoes, soft class
of a day. My red cat enters the coffin,
sleeps, wakes, finds recreation, inflate,
deflate, the tar-bedabbled rumory
lungs, strolls southward, the groin, and, pat,
hazards, sucker for the *bon mot*, the *cúpla*
well-chosen *focal* – 'Grizzled envoy mine,
how we scorned the semi-tone, our
motto ever – Cut the cackle.' Again
to doze, hasn't a care. Softish weather
in Pluais, men nodding, women anxious,
exquisitely, above their thrice-blessed shoes.

MY OLD CLOAK

Has to be I was sent to find
you, long-remainder'd God-forsaken
sometime intimate, I was, hay-seed
active in your seams has taken,
look, green tips – o, growthy gift,
a stannin wakeness overs me, banks
of nettle lean, gawk, as I snatch breath,
for these sainted firstlings give thanks,
beg pardon – I am – was – am
Intended of the loveliest ever born,
meadow, bog, wood, our spacious tram-
poline, we jived, the path little-worn
traced hand-in-hand, could do no wrong,
halted, *en travesti*, stocious by the spring.

WHY VEINS SHOW

In the hall with this young woman
(only just met, but we're about to part),
talking of the veins ferrying can after can
of sullied blood to the chamber'd heart.
'In the case of men,' I suggest, 'no veins
to be seen. With women quite the reverse.
Changing rooms,' I add, 'rowdy confines,
where else, put me on to it first.'
She takes me in. 'And why should that be,
do you fancy?' 'Haven't thought about it much.'
Cartographer's dream and redolent sea
of unabashed filigree, she lifts the latch,
opens the door, *slán*, and, as she leaves,
what sundered music that fair hair retrieves.

FELICITY

Few or none believe in my Chinese
cat, I know the know, and let it be,
some jewel, this dame, not a purchase,
not a present, one day appear'd, subtly,
so *gratin*, born marquee player, if ever
you live to meet one; scented mist (*stet*)
purls, continuous, from a canted ear,
dynastic tail, seat of memory, at rest,
haunches (by Brancusi) a like repose,
my Chinese sits by the mouse-hole,
hunter, *not* a hunter, to her very toes
satori, satin-wrapped in her Zen coracle,
could be studying gravel on Mars,
dreamin' a coup in second-hand cars.

CASTLETYMON
BRANCH
PH. 4524888

THE BLACK SWAN

Dear feathered Lilith (Mann, read
the story?), off kilter since the day
I did, wet-behind-the-lugs, prayed
at crooked intervals she'd spare me
but that's not Her Highness, if she has
your number. And knows when to show,
December moon will usher her, Empress
of The Small Hours, one with firm flow
of the river that's your uneven pulse,
nonpareil her grace, aplomb, haut-
eur, your liver screeches – 'One glance, else
melt-down' – but no, sorry, no,
she's absolute, path silver-scroll'd,
not a sound in either pendent world.

HER DAUGHTERS

One day her daughters will appear on
your doorstep, they'll want to know, have
to know, everything, how'd it happen,
every last detail; how memoried their grave
faces, you'll tell all, she, purely, swam
thru a glass door, sudden said Yes,
packed her duds, 'Bye, Dad, Mom,'
airport, seaport, land, Grandmother's
crockery coming to grief en route,
those poems she wrote in a rush, her
lemon soup, scones, ganseys, she taught
kids to swim, play piano, care
for bees, saved us both in a fog one day,
mere respite, those fogs make you pay.

INSTALLATION

Two-and-thirty tidy heaps on the floor
of the barn, from every county a clay
offering, no solitary sound here,
the large quiet pucker and roundelay;
strange on your pins, strangely view the heaps,
red clay and brown and yellow, blue
clay and olive, clatty clay, lumps,
Golden Vale clay for the Norman yahoo;
you are the tentative, the tired, pilgrim
arrived, might have removed your shoes;
casually purposeful, you roam,
find *your* patch, sticky drumlin, ooze
arrested; bury your hand, find a road,
iridescent, willowy, journey without end.

MEETING THE LAMB

Boreen after-dinner dander, sunset
alabhog, soft-warm, turn of the day,
a gap of light presents today's Must
Win, white to break the eye, stay
your foot, open a road, insist – 'Defer,
defer, Lamb's the tune, musician, in-
strument, morning's public secret stir,
one song too many for lots to sing;
daub now your door-post, nail
Lamb to the tree, Divilment God,
lips wet, curls amok, is out on bail,
in every virgin sky a red thread,
Dionysus carols, 'Cool your broth,
would ye, chill out, Drawky Death...'

THE MASK

Nel mezzo, meaning a wall, a cliff,
the whirlpool, I find it, crunch small
hours, splinc of the road, scan, tough
guy soft-in-the-horn, this elemental
plighted thing: it takes, owns you, then
and there, effortless, how blunt,
how polished, ebony, is it, the sheen
is ebony, chisel-scarred, slant,
announces – 'I'm yours. Time to choose.'
You gaze, locked in neural din of the flesh,
quietus. Gaze returned, full toss,
soul-brother come to settle your hash:
stand-off, road outside the house
where you were born, *nel mezzo*, small hours.

COMMENCEMENT NOTES

'Chariot without the wheel-rim,
we call poetry, and then, wheel-
rim without the chariot.' Mom
and Dad blanch, compose, kids double-
take. 'Among the letters, saraband S
is châtelaine and courtesan.' Someone
cocked up, big-time. (The poet's dress
leaves much to be desired.) 'Wine
is a rosin, true dancing stolen air' –
Chancellor gone ballistic, many worthy
parents dragon-eyed, *jeunesse dorée*
sit there, rumps in sweet disarray...
'Study to breathe, fashion time, prize
the berried sprig dancer's breath implies.'

THE SEAMSTRESS MUSING

I want prayers in special, please, for them
as nearly breaks outa the shell, never
stint those tremblers, make room,
you've met such, could be youse are
the like, the frecken'd ones gets almost
free, here they come, head, breasts,
an' then, for some rayson, does the light
hurt, courage fail, their fledglin' eyes,
curse o' God spacious deloother, un-
rayson, intrude, an' they're caught, frog
in a frost, poor craythurs, sink soon
enough into quiet, misfortune beg,
find it, an', ditherum, neglect the call,
their wings, wet wings, clogged in the shell.

YOUNG BEAUTY'S RECURRING DREAM

The fir tree stood between two mighty
beech, the swing hung from its lowest
branch, there she sat, and, too firmly,
clutched the ropes, no settled light
in the eye, she had, quick after a fashion,
found mime to protect this vagrant lack,
but such resorts could only briefly win
eye of the beholder, her desperate trick
laid bare, echo is echo, the world
no daw, 'Hurt mind one great pother
there,' said world, left her, imperill'd,
glued to the swing, 'tween which and whether,
your dream presented me her name,
the lawn, the swing, trees, cryin' shame.

HAVE YOU NO FEAR

Duskiss her hour, stay, sure, on the *qui*
vive, if you wish, it won't, in the wind-
up, help, turn a bend, there she
is, your sometime Princess, chair-bound,
hallooing from her verandah – 'He gave
sworn word, vamoosed. Scumbag fool!' –
ash-plant each hand, she drove
her theme – 'Doesn't fear of disaster kindle
you?' Nothing would do me but cross
her – 'Fear of disaster. Not really,
no.' *Lebide*. Watch her now redress
a cretin: to her feet, ash-plants thundery
against the floor invade, usurp, invest,
o, my Princess, streaky light to the west.

THE JESTER

Don't ever throw cold water
in his face, our mishap last night,
Old Adam transformed to Gauleiter,
betrayal, I'd now, *felix culpa*, right-
ify: praise, praise, your maverick
quilt of colours, duality's rainbow
spree, praise feckless caveat kick
of your cap-an'-bells, cow-horn flow
of light and seeing, wasn't I often told –
No one to play the cracked well as the wise;
come tap me with your bauble, fool-head
thingummy, posied with ass's ears,
baptise me, Master, as you were,
tempered in font, in mud, hot water.

THE OWL

I cherish most about your Christmas visit
its reticence. There I am, in-
ternal bleeding for a woman left,
you settle, fir tree, our eyes join;
that holds, half an hour, more,
December's spare light losing, game
loser, you there, balanced, your
dignity the purest thing, home
from home communion. The moon lifts,
our trust holds, tryst, tutelary
deference to light of reflection, shifts
of knowing beyond day's commissary.
You didn't fly away, that's not owl,
weren't there, simply, moon to the full.

LETTER

'Wrote you a letter,' she said, 'didn't
post it, kept it, there in my desk drawer.'
And again – 'Wrote you, didn't post
it, but I will now...' Neither letter
will I ever see, she-would-if-she-could-
but-she-can't-so-she-don't. It's not in
me to task her (she's divinely led)
for such velleities, begin to entertain
what these sequestered intimacies
might import, long on the road, *a stór*,
she-w'd-if-she, modulated sighs
resound, cadenza of the penn'd-never-
sent, I see it, hear it, we are *wired*,
last forever, don't they, melodies unheard.

NANNY

In her age she ran a post-office,
the hills, windy quarter, high, distant,
must visit her sometime, find purchase
in that child garden, did, spent
morning quiet, knock, for God's sake,
knock does it, hurt steps, curtain
aside, old woman, only the track
of her in it, once held, won
me, with her croon. The name. For-
gotten, has she? Peruses me, failing
eyes give nothing – wait – 'You're
the one'hand mimes act of writing,
I nod – we're joined – taboo alarms –
incantations, groundsel spells and charms.

MÁNA PÓIGE

means 'an itching of the lips portending
a kiss', never heard of it before?
Few have, it has too long been lying
dormant in the rumpled annals of *l'amour*;
it starts, trifle, knee-hollow or shin,
you'll come to recognise it, moves,
sweet particle, leisured and benign,
to the rib-cage (right side), leaves
that pagoda shade (you are required,
this module, merely to preserve calm),
shifts to the thigh-bone, left, tired
of wandering or, say it plain, home-
sick, leaps to the lips, dives to the breast;
now make the bed; she'll come; divest...

DRUMLIN PRAYER

Necklace of hills, thirty-mile-deep,
model, rebel, gallows, load o' whins;
bogs, stray-sod, acrostic; sip
your full of the lakes' ghost divarshions.
Temenos mine, suspicion's cradle,
conspiracy's whorehouse, ounce o' blood
before the churn o' buttermilk, your table
offers every spring, still of the wood,
mountain shelf, lowland – wet pout
of the hyacinth, planxty of whitethorn,
smell-a-fight divil's bit; and a bucket,
the suck-calf's slithery snout, moan.
Devious watershed, my windfall, my loom,
watch over me, w'd ye, the road home.

PICASSO (RIP) BY A WINDOW

A man soused in shadow walks the strand,
dog beside him, the full sea is labile
whisper; on wrack, some distance ahead,
discard ribs, pale blue, bugle
something to them, avid for reveille;
while the vase, brown, of flowers, on the corner
shelf is Iberian shrine – say
nothing – *voila!* – flowers stirring,
feathers now, becoming, rather, feathers
flowering in a brown vase – *chinng* –
it's all au naturel, this can be, yes,
a bird's arriving, *arriving*'s the word,
welcome the pert illimitable bird!

HOUSE ON A HILL

It is a madness, it's a must,
a graydle transpired in that kitchen,
so, hands on the sill, nose against
the fusty glass, look, loose pain
your ticket; you came to see, per-
chance to pray, turf fire ablaze,
Herself there to beckon, touch, offer
the love-feast, Paul Brady's voice –
'Once was a fellow named Arthur McBride...'
Your portion is a hostile frieze of damp,
mildew, tossed furniture, staid
neglect; grief the hearth, quenched lamp,
grief these cobwebs, woe the day,
day that's you, Love, distant in the clay.

THE SWAN

From a distance I could tell she was
messenger, where swan resides message
and messenger are one. A few metres
away, she hovers, the neatly folded page
flies to my feet. Mark her remove, her
castigation. No call, none, to read
the dispatch, but I take it from clover,
finger it, indicted, watch swan recede;
you are free – are you free? – you
are at liberty to keep this letter
on dusty shelf or fling on the fire, stew
of remorse either way. My soul's measure,
in a tall tower She waits, inmost kin,
nursing the beat of two hearts in one.

ARBOR VITAE

A tall tree, evergreen, beside
a second tall evergreen, intent
the pair, if you (yes?) feel waylaid
you should, already it's clear they want:
we study each other, now the trees
make their move, embrace: blent,
confront you, no haste, no unease,
call it wedlock and enhancement.
I watch and wait, let this develop,
a door, ground level, opens in the tree,
a door, a cunt, contagious *RSVP*.
This is not the vicar's garden party.
This is the grand invitation, I know.
And stand there, captive to the marrow.

EARTH-LIT

An abbey, brownstone, I am drawn
to enter. Teak-brown the large hall,
a monk, on his solitary stroll,
wears a cassock of Caledonian
brown, browns multiply; at one,
entirely, with himself, monk leaves on the table
a fish, also brown, and vulnerable
bravura Velasquez brown the curtain
he now draws, allowing more light,
a slew of browns, tanbark, hazel, cocoa,
mats, bowls, kneelers, the dun flow
is endless, swaddles a shy student.
Meet monk's eye – last leaf of the year,
marcescent, imponderable, your seer.

CONCERNING SOPHIE

You should have known Eve, fine lassie
next door, big heart on her sleeve,
a green apple, a tear; toiled slave
to Helen's fancies, boudoir patchouli,
poetry talk, flight of those panties
a Greek vase soirée; sinner, braved
Sister Mary, born sinners to save,
pastoral smile, serial Assumptions,
flare-path Annunciations; roamed,
Chevalier, with Sophie, o, Eve with a passion,
Helen grown wise, Mary down from
the mountain, I sit lost by the phone,
Midnight, Noon, Blight and Cure, Amaze,
working pulse that flagrant virgin kiss.

OCTOBER REVERIE

Christ: braw-year haw's a goner,
boor-tree anointed Princess of Dreck,
fauve leaf of my Lady Sycamore
branded a poxy Mardi Gras black.
Wish, wish I were Mahatma
Gandhi's ring-dove granddaughters
(gently we might engage) or a
Chinese Warrior free of the wars.
A shadow, carnal, moves about the garden,
master, you'd say, of futile excursions;
I've tried to imagine him at peace,
pondered an approach, sifted question.
But no. Why? From his starboard
hand dangles my white and lonesome head.

DAD

He's far more here now he's there,
frequently calls, has a word
or two, different man; wisdom beyond,
looks like, a larger tune, livelier;
plain he knows when there's bother,
precise contours of son's harsh need,
the answer and verifiable road
ahead, where I'll sprout, where wither.
Today he stood fornenst me, long spade
extended, spun handle, blade, fed
shaman circles into my famished eyes,
downed the teeming spade, touched my face –
'Short sorrow, Son, is a long sword' –
leaves me to the whistling wind.

TÓG BÓG Í

When they asked after you, I said –
'Ripening, she ripens, all the time
riper,' and a morning blossom spread,
we saw you among trees, rhyme
your ransom, day bright with showers,
wet-bright your apple of the sun.
Trim waiter appears, the soup, main
course, dessert, coffee, petits fours,
we talk of this and that, who's in,
who's out, bling, Beijing, missing thumb
of King Tut, we must banish Wotan,
Thor, any neb of thunder from the room;
this, it must, lands you at the table,
waiter, confused, murmurs – 'Madame – daughter' –
retreats in disorder, you do that to many,
Love, you there stitching your garments of plenty.

A PURE UNCLOUDED BLAZE

Brink of the one-strand river, Pat,
is where it's all happenin', damn
the hate much elsewhere, commend it
to your slew of children, Manannán
Mac Lir does exist, Pan is dead,
not he; we meet on the lower shore,
life full of meetings undeserved;
ardent white, head to toe, before
me stands yer boyo, jacket of shells,
culottes likewise, in his hand a trumpet
made of shells. Long look at
each other, then he smiles, caress
for the trumpet, playful envoy bow,
speaks – 'Like to hear it crow, would you?'

ONE SWALLOW EQUALS SUMMER

for Celine

Sh'd you ask me when it was decreed,
I'd say that day I found my prim bedroom
a clatter of birds, shook, you appeared
out of air. I ask – 'Where've they come
from?' As you, toughshit, answered – 'Eggs,'
I raise the invalid venetian blind,
one bird now, a swallow, magnified
for the hard of seeing, and the colours
cure for sore eyes: peacock blue, orient-
al red, faraway lure to the bird,
perched, nonchalant, on a bedpost,
measurless poise, sanctuary word.
The room took flight, we held hands.
Crick shed, I yield to psyche's demands.

COUNTRY MATTERS

Brambles galore, broadly Ladies' Garters,
writhe between you and satisfaction;
berry to die for, catwalk kickass
beautiful, ever Purgatory to attain.
Hands, arms, legs, belly, groin,
taking the hits, run for it, why not?
Read books instead, find distraction,
Amor Courtois, Morgan, Lancelot...
But ladybird on your wrist, left hand,
trills of Fall infusions, syrup, corn,
Neanderthal afters, cilial incand-
esence, caviar. This you'll spurn?
A pox on dentata seizures. Stretch. Mine.
In the mouth. Minge. No other wine.

BIVOUAC

Should you find yourself sleeping on top
of a cliff habitually, green grass
your pillow, candid sky, varied thump
of the sea an unruly hourglass,
do not postpone the obvious question.
Yet that impulse one can understand,
the grass green, the sky blue, saline
salubrious something to the gabby wind,
all the makings of an opiate, no
kiddin'. Slough it, Traveller, you're
there to a purpose, you are not below
our merciless radar of vacant future,
imperfect past, stern gerundive, shoe
leather. Rise. Shift it. Step into you.

THE ANTIC SEA

Beyond credence, I saw their sparkle lift
from the stony gable of Inishturk, seven
miles north, filly fountains in a sonsy
line, Versailles, I swear, unkempt compared;
they raced the rock – 'Leave yourself now,'
someone said – the seven fountains
depart the cliff-top, glide to the strait,
multiply by three, and, Terpsichore
in charge, southward tack, *corp-de-ballet*
épanoui, figure-dancing to render eye
immortal, until, shout only from me,
melding to tall mother-jet, a ravishment;
watch Regina Maris transmit Eternal Now,
wet laughter fly, slap my brow.

THE MOLE

I'm the pits. No one will give Her
the time of day. Alert, She comes
to touch, firm, my thrawneen shoulder;
we meet – casual high drama – on the stairs,
She ascending (last brush, miracle
encounter, foot of the stairs, my letter
in Her hand), now the house is canticle,
Canticle of Canticles, might She dwell here?
I stand beside Her. She's simply clothed,
is my north, south, east and west,
and the no-delay/never-a-hurry kind:
a singing motion frees Her left breast,
reveals the mole that proudly rears, says –
'Kiss, rest here, Man of Swithers and Swives.'

OLD MAN, WITH HAT

It was the worst season yet, it was
the fatality of down-the-street chat –
'And how's Herself?' 'Don't know.' 'Don't
know?' 'Herself is now somewhere else,
no more here will be.' The busted phrase,
yelp, 'I live from one day to the next,'
is flushed rubric, *matin, vesper, nones*;
till, darkest evening, remission's lent,
no charge: front avenue of child-
hood, an old man, Grand-Uncle
John from Finternagh, tossing ahead
his hat, watching it land, then fall
to his knees, kisses the ground, forward
again, reprise, reprise, and kiss the ground.

WHAT'S THE SNAKE STAND FOR?

Ask *The Belle of Amherst*. DHL. Ted
Hughes. Ask your mother. Let me tell
you of my tangle with her, Old
Slitherer, far more companionable
than we know. I've fled her – the bed,
townland, county, gobbet outa hell,
ancient cold, scales, fangy quiet, skewed
whisper; takes the longest day, a single
road, unfolded fear, to kiss the snake,
takes vows, libation, takes the back
or the lash, such season'd timber. But once
you realise snake *wants* the kiss,
also bereft, it's an affair, like any other,
only different, lasting, here, everywhere.

CATTLE, ERRISLANNIN

She was beautiful, I couldn't see
the altar for the trees, now and again
I glimpsed, worshipped, her drowsy mien,
but my passion was a cupboard, noisy,
hair, hanks of it, dissolving in the rain,
and a red cat, o, such a purblind red,
soft-footed Guarantor of Self-Combustion,
and slick Controller of The Walking Dead;
no great surprise then, back in Dublin,
we're informed my ghost's been active –
to great distress of cherished *Limousin* –
the month since we'd taken our leave.
She looked at me, beloved phantom bride,
looked thru me, listened, heard the music fled.

SALOME, JOHN, SHE SAYS

'Herod's the Protector, poor Herodias
a bruise, dirty John your terrorist
penn'd in the basement, and I want
Salome to have a Big Sis,
that sane encumbrance.' I nod –
'Go on.' 'I love some costive Miriam
stating the law to Patty Hearst. And
I'll have a Pandarus, let him
be castrato, away with your helden-tenor,
your counter-tenor, your – and we need
a child' – *scherzando* her eyes – 'The child
John and Salome never had.' Dear
God, I adored her tang of misrule.
Next thing tells me she's to marry a fool.

RAIN

is a woman, surely, compleat lover,
I mean, to be sure, rain at its best,
some move early, more late, to discover
it, lucky eyes a help, palimpsest
riddles or (imagine!) last blaze
of Love's latest breath. The Old People
spoke of 'kissing rain', stirred the phrase
above colcannon, bacon, fosey-feeble
turf fires, you knew, skin don't deceive,
what they meant: distilled surround of mizzle-
moidered shifts, mantillas, toccata veil
of precipitation, tears of angels, sieved,
a moisture, lisping – 'Win this Haunted Lovely,
love her, win her, you must truly haunted be.'

HOMECOMING

From an upstairs window, upstairs
always *droch scéal* with me, basement
another trap (where, where, blossoms
may I find, what, Christ, I'm meant
to be), steam pours – or smoke – hyper-
ventilation, take your pick; in the cafe
next door, prideful plus, by the counter,
a male mannequin, headless stray,
wrapped in tinfoil, is he for the oven?
I shouldn't have fled the coop, stealth
always loss. 'Romance is a man,'
waiter recites, 'without soul to drive to death.'
Holy Shit, on the doorstep a copper helmet,
that helmet blazes, *take it, man, take it*!

OULD SEGOTIAS
for MH

When you called to tell me of your
dream – a friend takes you to a house
where you find in the garden two hares,
a big, a little, both engrossing, the pair
smoking roll-ups – on the spot I am
back among my old compantors,
urbane *boulevardiers*, discovery of them,
so difficult their arcana to learn, since
they're the night, the cunt, the foamy womb;
how do you shape obeisances,
how, Plato, meet that rakish incense
rising from their roll-ups, come
clean with them, walk to meet the heron,
Christ-bird, with spear, how may we learn?

COLLEGE

I twice saw Paddy Kavanagh plain:
Stephen's Green, pet day, hat he wore
well on the Kildare side saying –
'Why be academic about laughter?'
The big-bone shoulders added – 'I'm
on my own, no other place to be.' The shoes
untied made clear – 'My love lives,
She'll never die, say hello to Her in
your third eye. I am, by the way, bookie
bound, insider knowledge, Chester
three-thirty, palamino Mercury
to win' – a wave, going – 'comic canter.'
Then there was The Physics Theatre,
night he led us to The Holy Door.

THE GATHERING

They all came to Swift's funeral
but, way of the world, there were
Prime Mourners, and, for good measure,
never those you'd expect: frail
slip of a thing, name Delia Somebody,
threw the first handful, he'd snarl'd at her
outside of an inn, summer of twenty-four;
an immature black-an'-white collie,
ownerless, loosed a Last Post
to woo the clouds; and that shapely green
bottle stepped up, the one, elixir *bleaist*,
from his remember'd dream, she went down
with him, goblin that fairly teas'd, aye,
mocked him, from The Deanery cellar clay.

SIGNS

Coarse weight of sleep shifts a bit,
thank you, I find dawn has
arrived, *pointilliste*, kindly enters,
as kindly plays, my spoon of the breast;
the white door ajar makes its
third visit, mite only ajar, I'm
asked to welcome a male figure: his
cassock's in gentle motion, the same
note, head to toe, outline, in essence,
intaglio. And, no surprise, have a go
at this lonesome crust, o, Leonardo,
on a long table, relic of the feast;
I study that crust, it has tales to tell.
Talk to it, my words inaudible.

GROTOWSKI

Word comes up the turnpike, he's in
Kent State tonight, young blood still
dark on that ravished ground, a sin,
mortal, protest against the daily kill
of kids in hamlets far away. Lecture
Hall 101, the true Polish prophet,
cap-a-pie in black, chain smoker,
tireless motion asks you to share,
augment, his missionary troth,
enroll. He said, 'Listen, theatre, listen,
it's play, you've seen, haven't you, been,
songful children playing toward night,
hardly know you're playing, you are
tho'. They have you on radar. They stare.'

BECOMING SMOKE

I meet smoke a deal lately, goes
with age, perhaps, see it rising from
a furrow, felled tree, flower's
petal, smoke, fumes of incense, steam.
I watch the collogin' curls at play,
they're so salient, wise beyond reason,
profit or loss, without hurry, can say
where they're going, flirt with the bone
in your eye, diffuse, reappear, *relate*,
that's their shtick, I can tell you,
no scarcity of eros where they mate,
they've been – and back – they rue
nothing. See them, I go quiet, stand,
become my clumsy gossoon hand.

SHEBA & THE GAEL

She's been sighted in Killinkere,
Tullamore, Roscommon, Cavan Town,
at it everywhere, see that pillar-
box, sconsed there now, snug, gain-
fully (cat-nap) employed: mere 'figment',
Official Sources say, 'entirely a function
of changing immigration patterns.' Scent
there the woe-the-day she causes men,
this Hoyden of Penumbra, with her seven
tongues, motionless ambages, left hand
ten-fingered as of right, dolphin
sighs, elastic ampussy-and –
coitus, sez she – 'Avec nous, reee-joice,
Irelan' unfree nevah be at peace.'

TRAVEL GUIDE

The name of this island? Call it
what you will. Longitude? Latitude?
You'll find out. It will let
you know you now tread
where all matters. In for a dunt? Yes,
there are animals untamed, go with that,
look for smitten light, prepare to address
a change of eye-colour, violet,
turquoise, often wine-green; don't
be frightened, look for singular
laughter, featherweight, a coral glint,
look for Chinese lanterns, bells, more,
look for at last learning to swim
Her stroke. The Soul Woman. Come.

WANDERING

They gave me the run of the pulpit,
white tub of childhood, a captive
audience, nave and chancel. Words arrive,
the coffin listened, it was all right;
in the cemetery I made the bishop
a present of the book I'd read from,
he fingered the cover, recent slim volume,
gave thanks. So. Decent chap.
The hotel dining-room, they were
there from hell to Connacht, in their best,
and they all had stories, must confer
on the storyteller their stories. *Must.*
Meal over, I drift. Telemachus
appears. Firm arms about me. Yes.

THE GIFT

Willendorf, de Milo, for you the sigh,
awake to find a breast I've grown,
left breast, *quelle surprise*, then I
twig: we've courted for an aeon.
Beautiful, beautiful, beautiful breast,
sacred and unholy wonder, I touch her
with my right hand, shy, modest,
thrifty, and, man, so cradle/warm the stir,
the lifts, sashays; next the bold nipple
seeks a finger, finds, lippy princ-
ess mine, ditty's allegro, tell
me this isn't madness, or 'Once
upon a time', so glad it's the left,
don't quite know why, more heft?

THE GENERAL'S MID-LIFE CRISIS

He had the snake dream, eagle dream,
dreamt the herald's golden staff, put
on women's clothes, fled by night
to the court of The Persian King, flame
his forehead. Xerxes listened, half-listened,
arranged matters – 'Pray be our guest,
Themistocles' – appointed him Chief Priest
of The Temple: laud we the Gods, basin,
beast, sacrifice, he minister'd thirty
assiduous years. How much is real?
Xerxes poker-puss'd, he'd seen it all,
over and over. Life. Seldom purty.
The wars again. 'We need your aid,
Themistocles.' He drank bull's blood.

WINDFALL

It waylays me in the turf-shed, quite
at its ease. *For you.* A red book,
one glance reveals the only uncut
page to be the last. I don't lack
a knife, hunter's knife, ivory handle,
the father gave me in the long ago –
why is there in me such a spill
of joy? (Last night I met a window
with a mountain view, shining bens.)
Insert the knife, take it, please, slowly,
for the fine pleasure of the act, paper's
giving, warbling, before the blade, featly;
it's April 23rd, friends, I scent Avon,
scent a Goodly Knight, a dragon slain.

WARD 13

Wind sieves light, a daylight moon,
salvific Sister, and my friends, expected,
I suppose, good to see them again,
we must, an edict, go where we are led;
says The Fat, smirky – 'Baa-Baa, Black
Sheep, has he any wool?' They always
look the spit of themselves. Content to take
my hour, I watch light sieve the breeze,
I'm eager. 'Well, well, Black Sheep,'
sings The Lean, 'e'er a bale o' wool?'
All my miching cells take a sweet lep,
an' I holler – 'Yessir, yessir, three bags full,
one for The Mistress, one for The Maid, & one
for The Litle Boy lives down the lane.'

CATHAL BUÍ

Mind the day you wrote your first
poem, you no age, uneasy by the lake,
October it was, not that far off dusk,
an' you clock me bittern, roostin', whisht,
on a reed, look again, duck low
in the rushes, hould yer hoult, bittern,
bittern is *plaitin'* the reeds, weavin',
d'ye mind, a ladder, perch, a yalla-
lemon ladder, goes unnoticed nearly,
one with hummin' yallas of the reed
bed, his plumage, your yalla head;
from a swoon of yalla, olives, strawberry
blonde, you watch: child, bittern, shore,
ordain the miracle, the fish in store.

TELEMACHUS

sleepwalking, lands in my bed, a
woman, woman-trouble, what else,
decibel by decibel my body counts his
distress, she sleeps a few rooms away,
wonder if she's awake, wants him but
it's over, winged confusion to
the pair, so I rouse him, do
I, say – what? The Life so short,
The Love so hard to learn, Love must be
thronèd, slave, Love must... The apartment
still, night a distance, blood so filmy,
maybe, could be, we're all somnambulist...
She's a star, as is he, but it's no-win,
we lie here, far away flowers in a garden.

THE LITTLE BOY WHO

No one speaks of him because he's
it, let our maiden meeting stand for
them all: daylight or thereabouts,
enter a garden, old, full of weather,
a woman and her daughter move away
yet that's invitation, they're allowing
space – for the garden pool. I know
my life's in this cut, cursive knowing;
now a dog surfaces, pointer,
plein-air white and brown, swims
ashore, and is The Boy, Ecce, who strolls,
a dancer's foot, where wild orchids flare,
turn of the hand, breath, gathers pollen,
pollen, pollen gathers, ambles on...

THE SMILE

Francis Bacon, artist, confess'd he'd
spent a lifetime trying to paint the smile,
and you ask the tongs again, house still,
from where the smile? Grandmother told
me (didn't often smile, when she did
she wheezed) at an early age, I can't
but ring the day, told me that gift
was 'dear bought', her counsel bright blade
in a warty paw. I'd no notion
what she meant, some sense, jiggedy,
now. '*Dear bought*, Child,' directs me
to that Greek note solvent in our pain;
to get, get and hold it, you give all,
and *They* give you a voice, a subject's smile.

WHAT HAPPENED SWEENEY

Rise up, lovely Sweeney, and give us nowt
but hay – you threw the book at them,
hari kari for a short cut, and out
the door in smoke – Me Ould Flame!
Where to go? The timber. You made secret
galleries your home, beech for runes,
the may for light, elm for rot. Wrens
told you – 'Eat the tree, Sweeney, *eat*
her' – calorific firestorm, *à tout à l'heure*,
Alligator! Gourmet Wild One,
you listened to the animals, regular,
the boar, the hare, the *matin*-blue fawn.
Loved winter too. And lov'd, here your
molten cross, lov'd an only daughter.

THE DIVINE CHILD

posits male, I know, lose a limb
or two, would ye, times a-changin',
have you met Ms Livin' Danger,
here's a damsel knows her hour is come;
remark, please, a rare ton, *tsigane*
savvy, mapped your palm an' you
mere glint; topless eye, no statue
safe; Met. Office – *and* the hurricane.
She's *amárach*. But what most I
must commemorate is mise-en-scene
parfait: on my lap, by the fire, hellion,
dove, Godiva's blue eye, pecan-pie:
the spark flies to single a strand of her
laughing hair, lifts, homes to the fire.

APOSTOLIC SUCCESSION

Moore and AE I want among
my Twelve Apostles for the day they *did*
Newgrange, *l'admirable* Moore keeping
a distance, AE digitally tuned
to The Other Side, the gaiter'd clergymen,
two, from Purtydown, parables of the kirky,
Aonghus a breeze, Etain telling a lie,
the ineluctable hours shaping to an
omega, foetal mounds a clockin' hen,
that moment, evening come, our cyclists,
Drogheda-bent, meet the *cailín*, the dozen
cows, to a bronzed silence let her pass.
Speak someone. Moore – 'Who was she?'
'Before the tumuli,' AE supplied, 'she was.'

VISITOR

I'm still uncertain if she was. West
Cavan, Shannon Pot country, woman
at the door. 'Come in.' Hag or Queen,
you're askin' me, gave her a chair to sit.
Tay. Thru the window the view led
to Glan Gap. 'Tell me about Glan,'
I asked. Taste the look of her, sand-
stone or mist. 'Twas never conquered.'
Suckin' tay. Love her sibilant eye,
restless foot, all-weather stain,
pax pro tem. We lounge in by-an'-by,
let contentment tease us from its skein.
'And *The Magic Cow of Glan*?' Said
nothing. Spoke – 'She gave till she bled.'

LA PUISSANCE

It happens at tremendous speed –
if there's such a thing as time where
They flourish – she's stripped, combat-mode,
carries a wand, meets the black bear;
it's clear she knows what she's about,
dances, even, as she goes to her
ritual; wand to the bear's mouth,
tap-tap, she removes tooth after
tooth, I'm happy to be dumb pupil
in her class-room, enroll'd willy-nilly,
soon a fistful of teeth, the bear her butty.
She turns to me, presents the haul –
'Here you go' – teacher's voice – 'You know
what to do now, don't you?' And they go.

SALAD STAYS

I am impaled, we're teens,
follow him like a pup, grimly aware
of Purgatory, dreaming of sins
would yield Paradise. Together or
apart, I'm inert, surly, tight-ass'd,
kithogue-culchie. This be love? Only
Cupid knows. The hots. Eventually,
it's agreed, he'll 'overnight', deal toned
carefully to seem acausal, all
in a day's idling. My pulse is scant.
He? I couldn't, for gold, make that call.
Consent? Let it happen. *Au lit!*
His every part stiff with virgin fright,
how could I? Morning, surly, he left.

ADOLF UBIQUITY

I'd begun to think we were close,
Eagle and I. Sure, we have a history,
sky-road from his disdain to lofty
benevolence of late, I bow to his sus,
go that far. Now, full moon, he shows
outside the house, boss-man, minatory,
with *Ku Klux* veiled head, eye-
slits *à la mode*, and motionless
to sour your spit. I sweat piss, go
to meet him, let's have it out.
'Why this parade?' He's so cool, no
fuss, and, not in soot, one to shout.
'You clothed me thus,' replies Eagle,
'I'm here to your call. *Sieg Heil!*'

MÉNAGE-À-TROIS, PRESQUE

My *Beauty From The Beyond*'s makin' out
with *Dear Unlawful Wedded*, somehow
knew it would come to this. *Good lay,
how are ye*, they dissolve, bedew the flagrant,
tongues of fire, silk, Tokay, I could feel
deserted, do, endure until *Belle Beyond*
swivels to me – Cleopatra plenitude,
persuasions, erotica of chakra crawl
and coil and – Kamadeva, 'tis sweet to be.
The scripted next pairing's hungry flesh? –
sin é! – harmony to be wrapped in *Herself*,
our turn, apprentice human lips the *entrée*
to *Triple Whammy* – shit – 'Later' – a yawn,
a sigh. Brimful slumber. And you're alone.

SPRING DAY

Meet him regular on my daily tramp,
he's the bit slow, never says much, today
he shows out of a pot-hole, touché
of apparition, head down, slow step;
he's approaching with barrow, call him brute
pushing barrow, piled with daffodils:
dung, turf, Godsends, his resolute
step says, benisons of an April
showery day, he'll do whatever he's
bid. I've overlooked a messenger
status – my feckless eye – might be his:
on a tuppeny-ha'penny dray, Proser-
pina's blossoms, and I am still'd, yea,
quenched, *Timor mortis conturbat me*.

REYNARD MEANS STRONG IN COUNSEL

Been close for years, on, off, on
again, my scarred potato-heart swerves
from the truth his tenderness defines,
mana, right communion, proper pain
of learning. Latest twist: discover him
wasted in the attic. Take flight. Return
next day. Better. Some movement. Some.
I leave food, OD on wine...
Sequel: a walled garden, back to himself,
largely – but, as I arrive, he exits;
a glance, gone, to notable resolve.
I waver in that abundant green recess,
no waiver, take the hit – *Amor
vincit omnia*. Stand. Stand there.

BLUEBEARD, PAST IT

You thought to find him zimmer-fram'd
bag o' bones in some Hospice of The Dying.
Really? Who's that, Table Nine, chatting
the young beauty, who listens, thrill'd,
as he prescribes, with panhandle
plawmas, The Flaming Door we
must abide if we're to meet the world,
two worlds, strokes her hand (shortly
the first pear-drop tear), he's telling
salt truth, that's why she listens, why
flushes, as the fondly sculpted ring-
lets fray, look, again, she's fit to cry...
Is he fake? On his bed, she'll tell you,
a leopard's paw. Polish'd memento. So?

) WHAT HAPPENED THE COBBLER (

One morning, sunlight lilting caress
on a tin plate, he met the vision, took
flight, set it all down, the flow was
torrent, wife, kids, forgotten, work
forgotten, God moves in circles, and those
circles move thru Glowing Hills, music
revels in the arc, circumference
is centre, not a crust to eat, shack
roofless, can this hold? The German
baron came. Subsidies! Wife content,
kids' lean cheeks rounded, hint
of the rubicund. On the cobbler's stone
a name, between a circle's ruins,
brackets reversed, bits, backassways.

IMAGINE, ONE ALONE

Marina Tsvetayeva, dancing *ex*
cathedra her bebop and only vein,
declares, get this, 'imagine' and 'one alone'
to be the same – the knees racket as
I listen to you, Silver Age hobo queen;
'to imagine,' she says, 'is already proof
of aloneness,' pluck that lemon leaf
from the tree, wash it down with wine
vinegar, 'proof of aloneness, source,
and recompense.' Marina, back from
wherever, with it said, adds, 'Just as
aloneness is Imagination's loom
and single field of action.' One high
altar: before you reach it, lives go by.

BEREAVED

What is it about funerals, have you
noticed, the daughter of the house *must*
make love, no faux-modesty about
it, crowd steadies, piper gerns *Salut*,
a casually bevelled glance makes clear
where you stand in her predilections,
she's never, cross my heart, looked more
beautiful, joyful, even, mourner veils
will do that, but, in truth, it's her –
what? – proud ride of those hips, grace
beneath unending 'Sorry-fors' – demise,
simply that? – *immortelle* rondo of the future...
Sudden, it's night, two naked, a room;
she opens to you, triumphant every limb.

THE FIFTIES

There were summers then, they passed us
by, our bibs wet, allegiance to the sour
tit total, how to gather, we'd ponder,
those uncontainable July evenings;
the Pelican House van, young nurses
in tow, aroused interest, go for
it; so to the favoured town, our
aspirant bodies washed, tight gazes
towards we knew not what, and
no tomorrow, how we havered to the touch
of those Nightingales, this refined hand
of Venus, tourniquet, needle, rich
surrender of blood, a dark measure, stream-
ing slowly from some faery realm.

BEQUEST, SORTOV

Commended highly to ye held dear:
animals of soul, persuade these
to your acre, *glic* fox, rutful hare,
badger's slouch, stoat, a pale horse
riderless pro tem; birds of intelligence,
eagle, goldcrest, long-tailed harrier
hen, she knows more nor her prayers,
the dove so easy for to wound, and spare
time for the hawk – he'll teach you to fly
on one transparent wing; fish of heart,
every shell-fish Europa kisses, John Dory –
thumb'd of The Lord, eels, compass lit,
gillamíní; also plants of dream, remember,
cherish, notably, yon Purple Flower.

RITE

Don't know if this will work for
you, worked for me, *crise* per-
ilous; old women, mostly, I'd heard tell
of the black-handled knife, it was core
signal, got hold of one, thereafter
followed myself; knew the hearth, real
presence, must figure, said a prayer, fell
to my knees there, sank blade in the floor;
a quiet hummed; fist tight on that black
handle, I tasted the house stronger at once,
shadow pushed back, whisper/flick
of a clement shower; still on my tardy knees,
head lowered, I glimpse dancing feet
next me. *She's* here. Exultant, I wait.

THE STONE

I hardly know of silence since the stone
spoke, advised – 'If you'd know sea-level,
rest on the beds of the sea,' and then –
'If you don't desire, where, where, tell
me, will your desire go?' Plantation
of fir, limestone lump. 'Who are you?'
I asked. Advisor, silently becoming kin,
returned – 'On your white door, two
pictures in welkin blue, a quill, a bird
in flight.' 'What's your name?' Good stone
looked thru me. 'What is it,' came again,
'of meat and moment you haven't yet heard?'
'How to knock on the door.' Finally from stone –
'I am the Cup, Cup-Bearer, and the Wine.'

HER CARE

The moment I gave assent, an ironing-
board, sweetly tailored fit, appeared,
the iron was in her hand, she checked
the temperature, already I'm lying
on the table, stripped, belly-up, storing
a mix of suspicion and contentment, heard
her woman-words, murmurs, never could
I have submitted but for those, a song
above the work; flitters of fury admit-
ted, she gauged them, flourished a sprinkler,
used delicately it became the bright
asperges of the hour; I had one terror,
the groin, but no, heart was the beast
at bay, old weasel heart, there the joust.

CHUTZPAH

I was stymied by the doorbell
stutters (peck-peck of a swallow, it
emerged), alongside failure to rumble
what next. The door, pliant, left
unlocked, swallow eases it ajar, makes
the house her own – doors wide, open
windows, skylights, the guest dismisses
them all, tours at will. When
you arrive, a wild serenity, the bird
and you are friends. 'Met before,
have you?' 'Often, other side of the wind.'
A purple ribbon, servant to your hair,
you toss to the bird. I look. And gaze.
Against the sky, a bird. A ribbon. Flares!

CATS

Their laden musk my tangled spoor,
I allow they must surely be inside me;
the black Tom, old Stiff-One-Eye,
no bullet works, my strike forever
his resurrection; and that Red Whore,
spare us, always there in the garden shade,
most fear'd of Caesar's legions wore
her on the Standard – Here, Lulu-Land
begins; the white cat's better news,
and not before time, see her daily,
a mouser, a matron, with firm views;
the blue cat I've seen once, a lady
inviolable, strolling a frantic street,
and I thought Yes. The Life. The Death.

THE WATCHMAKER

The silence took us, and the gloom fed
trance; cabin'd space did the rest,
abetted by the high counter, glass-topp'd,
which offered, and refused, a treasure-chest
of rudderless watches. Armstrong –
that pleased. Said little. Sufficient
eloquence the Granny specs. The King
Grandfather clock, watchful on its plinth
to the rere, we understood to be arm'd.
Hadn't, happily, yet come to pass, but
also knew Joe, one day, and soon, would
leap, soar, his high counter to frustrate
that oldest christened norn, The Wife with Knife.
Stunn'd, we watched The White Coats arrive.

KELLS, WINTER NIGHT

The hand-cart taking the steep hill
pushes itself. Riddle me that. Carries
straw, you clocked the straw – fuel
there, think you? All right, tell us
where it's going. It's climbin', has to be,
for The Round Tower. Full marks, top
of the class, buss the Mistress, now jump,
will you, self-propelled, straw, doughty
Tower? Bairn? Correct. This inroad,
multiracial Kells asleep or doing
the books or again miscegenating,
bespeaks the ever-dying, ever-resurrected
Son, the name's *Íosa*, listen, *Íosa*, *Íosa*
for wain at peace in sempiternal straw.

BIFTECK

On my plate – did I order un-
beknownst – badger steak, *bleu*, it
has no accompaniment, none
needed, native clout sufficient, and – wait,
wait – fingers on the flash cutlery,
I realise I *have* ordered it,
it's memorial, stage-lit,
friend badger, hoary stud, lately
seen crossing the spring morning garden,
dragging his six-pack back to the sett
after a night of it; theatre of that
slouch, driven skull, ageless moan:
the image holds – he padded away –
holds firm. Your steak. *Mangez. Bleu.*

SHORE DEAL

*Fionn's dream of suckling
two pup seals presaged his death.*
(Irish legend)

You'll hear them long, long, before
you see them, faraway impromptu
cups the ear, low, trembly news –
'Fall into the milk, Child, taste your
luck. A day set you'll give us suck.'
Then may you thrum to many meetings,
spindrift tutorials on the protean
strand, the Helpful Animal Selkie Love-
In, a cappella – 'Cream to the top if
you know how to churn; butter the crop,
if you don't know, learn.' And the bargain,
lest we forget – never was immersion
without a bargain – 'Ours be yours the time
to play: yours be ours the time to swim.'

REFLECTIONS IN A RHEUMY EYE

'Holdin' your hand's like milkin' a cow.'
'From where, tell us, the Rasputin smile?'
'Your love-sounds are tropical
birds.' 'Why, why so bereaved now?'
Old lag, slack features a cage,
scratches his crotch from under the table,
defines, doleful, punani pilgrimage –
'Daddy-Long-Legs footless on marble,'
listens, bothered ear, to Missy, The Maid,
who swears by the blue puss, blue fawn,
speaks, sings, of Time green in the blade,
pardons failure to greet The Unicorn,
adds, angel-eyed – 'You're rough trade.
Pilgrimage means a walk in the field.'

THE ASS

They've shown me The Glowing Hill, it
may not be described, and The Land of Others
melts the eye, and The Drum, yes, stript
me to a thread of hearing, trace
sufficient, tho', to pitch a song; The Ass –
here's the bind – Christ Ass, Golden,
Kerr's Big Ass, all the sodden donkeys
of my weanin', what is it they contain,
what am I being told when that bray
once more resounds? Pig-headed,
horny, humble, honoured servant of The Lord,
I'd a chance once to turn the key:
The Ass in bed, between us. There. Said
Ass – 'Wish to learn?' You slept. I fled.

A MOMENT COMES

Don't miss it, when the familiar stand
of beech – at last, at last, you notice it –
is at once old and young, wind
green and gold, and fledgeling dove, lit
interiorly, is passing by, and, precisely
the same hour, action by the window-pane,
a fly there, Freddie-Fat-an'-Friendly,
tugging at the glass – 'Look, I'm so thin,'
and, today the Feast of Simultaneity,
river, giving itself bobtail welcome,
declares the head of Orpheus to be,
a lip, a kiss, flotsam/jetsam, and then some,
it's the curls, tho, *douces*, take your
fancy, Raftery music, *amigo*, every curl.

CARE-HOME, HER BIRTHDAY

Avalon, they call it, hard to blame
them, what are we to do when
the hand of the potter shakes? Room
here, once a week, to solace June,
pixillated beauty, gobbles my stories
of talkative blackberries in the August
vat; Nell, suety of limb, haze
about her, and transfixed, *maladroit*,
the smile; Emir, starved with the cold,
has me kiss and kiss a bloated thumb;
and here's the kid sister, my grief untold.
'What age are you today?' 'Twenty-two.'
Once I was shown her might have been;
sundown, a doorstep, before me a queen.

OTHER TOMS, OTHER MOORES

Long ago, wide streets of the city
I met only downy young women,
now the collation's drystick old men.
X accosts me, just back from Italy,
would I admire his funereal tan?
Y, writer butty, lifts from the throng,
look, his hand's curious stiffening,
surgery scars, could be genetic, Sam
The Man had it. Enter Z, who text'd me
lately – 'Trip Down Under off. Doctors
forbid.' He departs – soundless, queasy,
head aloft – to dine alone with others.
Home. Demoted fireguard by the armchair,
focus on the grate, your attentive ember.

THE ASH

was no way shy yet from the word
Go, purdah our daylight, I gave her
the back of my hand, world my toaster,
Permanently Pensionable stepp'd
it out until, *They* don't forget, four-
o roundabout, she swoops. The car, I
was polishing the car, quick ear
to the ball-game (disaster). A mossy
cleft, hers, root level, traps my eye;
scallops, *fluirseach-flahoolach* handful,
this pitted earth halts as I glare, giddy,
cramp, stew: scallops opening, bell
tolling, clits, cunts, muscles, torn
lawless juices, insisting they be known.

BUT AS MALES THEY DISLIKED

'Mere breath of your name,' she phones,
'room's a slab of ice.' 'The heinous deed?'
'Guess, why don't ye?' Reflex thought is
where I slept last night, that broad
sloping meadow, serried flambeaux, green-
blue, of grown cabbage, a white butter-
fly proprietary above; down
my winter lane, a big Alsatian, Border
Guard, with spring to his tail, shouts – 'Gimme
five!' And, first light, rap on the words
women have bestowed me, corblimey –
aibhleog, rubato, désormais –
how women love, loving are, the sylvan vowel –
'Still there?' 'Suckin' diesel, Bella,'
I reply.

ARTHURIAN MATTERS

Thigh-wound at three-score-and-ten
brackets you as halting Fisher King,
prayer that it's casual misfortune
or, better, uterine, not worth a farthing.
My books, my books! Weeks with Percival
and Gawain, Blanchfleur, bleeding lance,
hags, hermits, questions – simplest of simple –
the hero will never ask, your lame dance
endures, Forests of Heathendom a mess
beyond navigation: you could be left
here for dead. Until, ex *gratia*, wet
Sabbath morning, lugging home the papers,
he meets me: ould goat, absorb'd wholly
in the breakfasting swans, nine-and-fifty,
beyond the main.

CALLING CARDS

They have again been active overnight,
this time the bathroom, busy palace
of evacuation, rubbing, paring, pills,
placebo potions. Reflecting December light
through reeded glass is a mantel clock,
cistern for plinth, you know those mantel
clocks' style, rise and fall of an able
hill, or, better, wave of the sea, no truck
with evasion; but night's tour-de-force
is the Chinese Lantern Plant, wasted,
on a shelf left of the looking-glass,
off-white requiem, the last word;
tattered pods, with heart-shaped scar
left by the seed, boldly enter my care.

THE KISS

I'd every hope I could upstage her,
crowd bought it too – late arrival,
fume of the outlaw, there was a murmur,
then stillness, how they parted, all
but touched the hem of my oilskin,
designer coup for an oven August day.
Wafted to her room, address the coffin.
Here she be, stranded wisp of grey,
rosary-bound blue hands on parade.
Kiss the corpse, valiant son. Slivers
of heliotrope, unhurried. Stoop. We kiss –
jump-start gallop churns my torpid blood –
that shuk ye an' yer still rockin' –
compose yourself, join mourners below,
wondering where you may this wreath bestow.

THE DOG

You do well to say *gratia* to The Dog,
it's been, no word of a lie, some journey,
learning to place the hand, readily,
in his mouth, discover teeth, spirals of tongue,
rookie path to his slope of The Wood.
Let's acknowledge betrayals by the score,
mark the day he snapped – 'Why not lead
me by the tail?' And response that summer
to your fly-blown spell as Circe's
toy-boy: Dog rambles by, rests a paw
on the raucous crotch, cool of his
paw, all the meadows a White Cow.
An hour ago he's here, lion-coloured,
the guide, near us a river, distant singing.

À VOTRE SERVICE

Death is a waiter, you've often heard,
found Him the other day above the taut
white sheet of my long-service bed,
ramasse-miettes in right hand, plate
in left, efficiently collecting the crumbs –
apparent to His expert eye – of a life-
time's feasting. *Momma mia*, silence
took, held me, all that fleshy strife
come to this. Never looked my way,
strict rather than chatty, I can confirm,
get the job done. Occurred to me
after – 'What's he do with the crumbs?'
No-brainer: all the l'avin's, yours, mine,
in ceaseless flow thru Demeter's mill again.